New Curriculum

Primary
Mathematics
Learn, practise and revise

Year 5

Mark Patmore
and Trevor Dixon

RISING★STARS

Rising Stars UK Ltd, 7 Hatchers Mews, Bermondsey Street, London SE1 3GS

www.risingstars-uk.com

Published 2013
Text, design and layout © Rising Stars UK Ltd.

Authors: Mark Patmore and Trevor Dixon
Maths consultant: Sarah-Anne Fernandes, Routes to Success, Sutton
Text design: Green Desert Ltd
Cover design: West 8 Design
Illustrations: Oxford Design and Illustrators
Publisher: Camilla Erskine

British Library Cataloguing in Publication Data.
A CIP record for this book is available from the British Library.

ISBN: 978-0-85769-676-2

Printed by Craft Print International Ltd, Singapore

Contents

How to get the best out of this book

Most chapters spread across four pages but some spread over two or three pages. All chapters focus on one topic and should help you to keep 'On track' and to 'Aim higher'.

Title: tells you the topic for the chapter.

What do you need to know? and **What will you learn?** tell you what you need to know before you start this chapter and what you are aiming to learn from this chapter.

Key facts: set out what you need to know and the ideas you need to understand fully.

Language: help to build up your mathematical vocabulary. Remember that some words mean one thing in everyday life and something more special in mathematics.

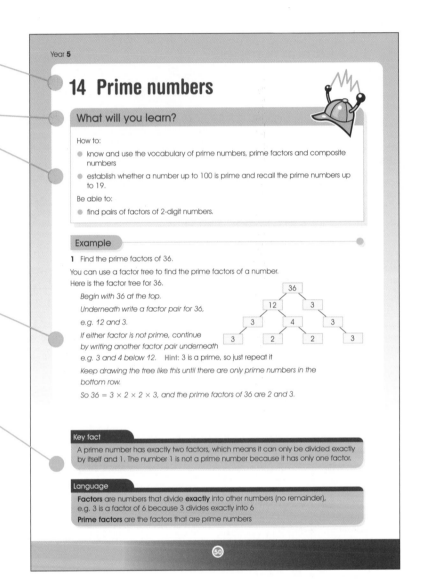

Follow these simple rules if you are using the book for revising.

1 Read each page carefully. Give yourself time to take in each idea.

2 Learn the key facts and ideas. Ask your teacher or mum, dad or the adult who looks after you if you need help.

3 Concentrate on the things you find more difficult.

4 Only work for about 20 minutes at a time. Take a break and then do more work.

If you get most of the **On track** questions right then you know you are working at the expected level for the year. Well done – that's brilliant! If you get most of the **Aiming high** questions right, you are working at the top of expectations for your year. You're doing really well!

The **Using and applying questions** are often more challenging and ask you to explain your answers or think of different ways of answering. The questions give you the chance to use and apply your learning by answering mathematical problems.

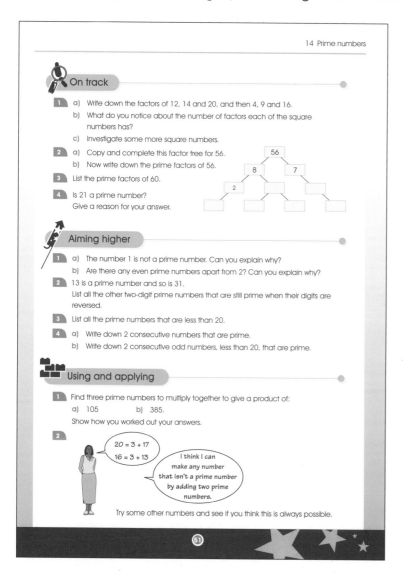

The answers to all the questions are in the pull-out section in the middle of this book.

Follow these simple rules if you want to know how well you are doing.

1 Work through the questions.

2 Check your answers with your teacher or using the answer booklet in the middle of the book.

3 Keep a record of how well you do.

4 Write down anything you are finding difficult and work through the chapter again to see if you can find the answer. If you are still finding it hard, ask your teacher for help.

1 Addition and subtraction with whole numbers and decimals

What will you learn?

How to:

● add and subtract whole numbers with more than 4 digits, using efficient written methods

● add and subtract numbers with up to 3 decimal places

● solve word problems involving addition and subtraction

● count up and down in 10s, 100s, 1000s.

I need to be able to:

● understand and use the place value headings for decimal numbers – units (u), tenths (t), hundredths (h), thousands (th)

● add and subtract numbers which are over 100

● recognise the different vocabulary for addition and subtraction

● check answers.

Examples

1 Find the total of: 1357 + 2468

In examples 1 and 2 remember to line up the numbers, starting with the units digits, as follows:

$$\begin{array}{r} 1\ 3\ 5\ 7 \\ +\ 2\ 4\ 6\ 8 \\ \hline 5 \\ {\scriptstyle 1} \end{array}$$

Start with the units column 7 + 8 = 15. Write 5 as the answer in the units column and the 1 (representing the 10) in the tens column.

$$\begin{array}{r} 1\ 3\ 5\ 7 \\ +\ 2\ 4\ 6\ 8 \\ \hline 2\ 5 \\ {\scriptstyle 1\ \ 1} \end{array}$$

Now add the digits in the tens column and include the 1 carried over from the first addition. 5 + 6 = 11 then add the 1 giving 12. Write 2 as the answer and the 1 in the hundreds column.

$$\begin{array}{r} 1\ 3\ 5\ 7 \\ +\ 2\ 4\ 6\ 8 \\ \hline 3\ 8\ 2\ 5 \\ {\scriptstyle 1\ \ 1} \end{array}$$

Carry on into the hundreds column 3 + 4 = 7 and add the 1 carried over making 8. And then add the 1 and 2 in the thousands column 1 + 2 = 3.

2 Work out: 58246 − 9789

$$\begin{array}{r} {}^4\cancel{5}\ {}^1\cancel{8}\ {}^1\cancel{2}\ {}^3\cancel{4}\ {}^16 \\ -\quad 9\ 7\ 8\ 9 \\ \hline 4\ 8\ 4\ 5\ 7 \end{array}$$

Start with the units column 6 − 9 gives a negative answer, so to avoid this change the 6 into 16 by taking a ten from the 4 tens. 9 from 16 = 7. Write 7 as the answer in the units column. Continue into the tens column 3 − 8 gives a negative answer so change the 3 into 13 by taking a ten from the column to the left. 13 − 8 = 5. Continue into the hundreds column and then into the thousands column.

Check that your answers are sensible – in example 1 the numbers are approximately 1400 + 2500, both numbers are rounded to the nearest 100, so the answer will be around 3900. In example 2 the numbers are approximately 60000 − 10000, both numbers rounded to the nearest 10000, so the answer will be around 50000.

● *In examples 3 and 4 you need to remember to line up the decimal points but then continue as you would with numbers without decimal points.*

3 What is: 24.543 + 9.678?

$$\begin{array}{r} 24.543 \\ +\ \ 9.678 \\ \hline 34.221 \end{array}$$

4 Calculate: 24.543 − 9.678

$$\begin{array}{r} 24.543 \\ -\ \ 9.678 \\ \hline 14.865 \end{array}$$

Check your answers. In Example 3, 24 .543 is about 24 and 9.678 is about 10 so the answer will approximately be 24 + 10 = 34. And in example 4 the answer will be roughly 24 − 10, which is 14.

Key facts

The value of each digit is given by its position or place.
The decimal point marks the division between whole numbers and the fraction part of a number, e.g. 4.786 is 4 units + 7 tenths + 8 hundredths + 6 thousandths.
Rounding numbers in calculations helps you check that your calculations are correct as in the examples above. It usually helps to round numbers to the nearest 5 or 10 or 100.

Language

Tenths (t) are $\frac{1}{10}$ of a unit

Hundredths (h) are $\frac{1}{100}$ of a unit

Thousandths (th) are $\frac{1}{1000}$ of a unit

To two decimal places means 'to the nearest hundredth'
Remember: the decimal fraction number names below zero are the same as the names above zero but with 'th' added.

[handwritten work at top of page:]
16333
26227 +
2560

5612 +
3456
9068

3322 +
7643
10a65

1111 +
999
1110

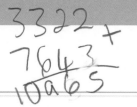

On track

1 Find the totals for these addition sums without using a calculator. First, though, write down a rough answer you could use to check your calculated answer.

a) 5612 + 3456 *9068* ✓   b) 3322 + 7643 *10a6s* ✓   c) 11111 + 999 *2110*

d) 16333 + 26227 *42560* ✓   e) 77777 + 14241 *9 2018* ✓   f) 12345 + 54321 *66666*

2 Work these out without using a calculator. First, though, write down a rough answer you could use to check your calculated answer.

a) 5612 – 3456 *2156* ✓   b) 7643 – 3322 *432r* c) 9004 – 478 *8526*

d) 26272 – 16345 *9927* ✓   e) 77777 – 14241 *635 36* f) 54321 – 12345 *41996* ✗

3 How do you find the difference between these pairs of numbers? Write down the difference you calculate.   *Minuce them*

a) 4567 and 4367   *200* ✓   b) 7499 and 7609   *110* ✓   c) 2943 and 2643   *300* ✓

4 Work these out without using a calculator.

a) 3 + 0.005   b) 0.011 + 0.999   c) 16.333 + 2.622

5 Work these out without using a calculator:

a) 3 – 0.005   b) 1 – 0.999   c) 16.333 – 2.628

6 What are the next two numbers in these number sequences?:

a) 400, 500, 600, *700, 800* ✓

b) 1030, 1130, 1230, *1330 1430* ✓

c) 9988, 8988, 7988, *6988 5988* ✓

Aiming higher

1 Write down 5 addition sums which all have the answer 1.25.

2 Write in two numbers, each greater than 50, to complete this subtraction:

$$\square\square - \square\square = 37$$

3 Write down the four numbers to make this subtraction correct:

```
  6  2  4  7
- □  □  □  □
  ----------
  3  4  9  5
```

4 Which number is wrong in the following sequence?

14 360,   14 460,   14 550,   14 660,   14 760

What should the number be? 14560

5 John says that 4200 + 10 000 = 5200. Is he correct?

Using and applying

1 a) What is the smallest 3-digit number?

   b) What is the largest 3-digit number?

   c) What is the difference between these two numbers?

2 Copy out this grid and then solve this cross number puzzle.

13 458 7
11 7
4 56

A 27			B	C			
D	E		F		G		
	H	I					
				J		K	
		L	M			N	P
Q					R		

Clues Across:

A 14.64 + 12.36

B 13 458 + 11 775 + 456

D 99 − 12.68 − 3.32

F 216.3 + 52.64 − 20.94

H 10 + 10.8 + 100.2

J 12 345 − 12 118

L 1000 − 35

N 27.468 − 0.222 − 3.246

Q 70 000 + 3800 + 9

R 1.11 + 2.22 + 3.33 + 4.44 + 3.90

Clues Down:

A 30000 − 29712

C 600 − 96

E 4000 − 3969

F 1 + 2 + 3 + 4 + 5 + 6

G 250 + 250 + 250 + 52.00

I 500 − 201

J 3000 − 2975

K 32 + 32.13 + 6.07 + 1.604 + 0.196

M 666.66 − 66.66

P the smallest number you can make using the digits 5, 4 and 4

3 Write down any 3-digit number with its first digit at least 2 more than the last digit.

643

- Reverse the order of the digits   346
- Find the difference between the two numbers 643 − 346 =   297
- Reverse the order of the digits   792
- Add the 2 numbers   792 + 297 =   1089

Try this with some 3 digit numbers of your own. What happens?

2 Negative numbers

What will you learn?

I know how to:

- interpret negative numbers in context
- count forwards and backwards with positive and negative whole numbers through zero.

I need to be able to:

- remember that numbers less than zero are negative
- count up from zero or any other number and count down below zero.

You may find this picture of a thermometer useful. You could also use the scale as a number line.

Examples

1 What is:

a)   10 − 15   **b)**   −3 + 5?   **c)**   −15 + 10?

a) If you count 15 down a number line from 10 you will finish on −5.

b) Count up 5 from −3 the answer is 2.

c) Count up 10 from −15 the answer is −5.

2 Write this list of temperatures in order, lowest first.

−12 °C,   17 °C,   0 °C,   −0.5 °C,   13 °C

−12 °C,   −0.5 °C,   0 °C,   13 °C,   17 °C

Key facts

Negative numbers are shown to the left of zero on a horizontal number line and below zero on a vertical number line.

If you count along a number line from left to right or bottom to top, the numbers get bigger.

Language

Positive numbers   numbers greater than zero
Negative numbers   numbers less than zero

On track

1 Write down the numbers marked a), b), c), d) and e) on this number line.

2 a) What is the temperature on this thermometer? $25°C$ ✓

b) The temperature falls by 27°C. What will the temperature be? $-4°C$ ✓

3 a) What is the temperature on this thermometer?

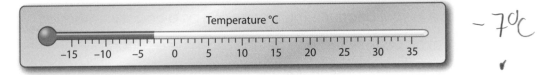

$-7°C$

b) The temperature rises by 17°C. What will the temperature be? $23°C$

4 The temperature in Moscow in December is –5°C.

a) In London the average temperature in December is 6°C. What is the difference between the Moscow and London temperatures? $11°C$ ✓

b) In Sydney the average temperature in December is 21°C. What is $26°C$ the difference between the Moscow and Sydney temperatures?

Aiming higher

1 Copy the table and fill in the gaps.

	Starting temperature	Change	Final temperature
a)	–6°C	a rise of 3 degrees	– 3°C
b)	7°C	a fall of 15 degrees	– 8°C
c)		a rise of 2 degrees	5°C
d)	4°C		–2°C
e)	–3°C		2°C
f)		a fall of 8 degrees	–4°C
g)	–12°C		12°C
h)	–8°C		5°C
i)		a rise of 15 degrees	7°C

2 If you have a bank account, sometimes you can take out more money than you have in your account. This is recorded as a negative number.

a) Ali looks at his bank statement. He has £75 in his account.

He puts £55 in and takes £150.

How much does he have left?

b) Sam looks at his statement. He has –£25 in his account.

He puts £20 in and takes out £30.

How much does he have left?

c) Manisha looks at her statement. She has –£45 in her account.

She puts £110 in and takes out £80.

How much does she have left?

d) Daisy looks at her statement. She has –£40 in her account.

She puts in £15 and takes out £50.

How much does she have left?

3 What is the missing number in these number sentences?

a) $5 - \boxed{} = -9$ b) $7 - \boxed{} = -15$

c) $\boxed{} + 6 = -4$ d) $\boxed{} - 6 = -20$

e) $\boxed{} + 5 - 6 = -4$ f) $\boxed{} - 7 - 5 = -9$

g) $8 - \boxed{} + 5 = -7$ h) $\boxed{} - 4 - 3 = -20$

Using and applying

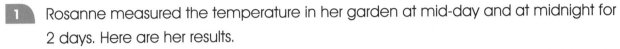

1 Rosanne measured the temperature in her garden at mid-day and at midnight for 2 days. Here are her results.

Day	Saturday mid-day	Saturday midnight	Sunday mid-day	Sunday midnight
Temperature °C	7	–2	3	–5

a) How much did the temperature change between each reading?

b) How many degrees are there between the highest temperature and the lowest temperature?

c) At midday on Monday the temperature was 7 °C warmer than at midnight on Sunday. What the temperature at midday on Monday?

2 This table lists the heights and depths of six places above or below sea level.

Place	Heights and Depths (metres)
Mount Everest	8863
Bottom of Lake Baikal	–1484
Bottom of the Dead Sea	–792
Ben Nevis	1344
Marianas Trench	–11022
Mont Blanc	4807

a) Put the measurements in order, highest first.

b) What is the difference in metres between the highest and lowest places?

3 Roman numerals

What will you learn?

How to:

- read Roman numerals to 1000 (M) and recognise years written in Roman numerals.

I need to be able to:

- work systematically
- add numbers.

Background

You may have already met Roman numbers and numerals. You will see them around you: on clock faces and watches, on programmes on television, in books.

You may find this table helpful.

In the number system we use today, the position of a digit in a number shows its value: for example, 26 stands for 2 tens and 6 units.

Roman numerals were abbreviations for writing down and recording numbers. The system included simple addition: although the key figures (I = 1, V = 5, X = 10, L = 50, C = 100, D = 500, M = 1000) could stand alone, placing them side by side usually meant addition.

So XV = 10 + 5 = 15; LXI = 50 + 10 + 1 = 61; CLXXXVII = 100 + 50 + 10 + 10 + 10 + 5 + 1 + 1 = 187.

However, the Roman rule for subtraction made everything more complicated. Every figure to the **left** of a figure of higher value had to be subtracted from it, so that IV = 5 – 1 = 4; XC = 100 – 10 = 90; and XIX = 10 + 9 = 19.

Common Roman numeral	Our numbers
I	1
II	2
III	3
IV	4
V	5
VI	6
VII	7
VIII	8
IX	9
X	10
XI	11
XII	12
XV	15
XX	20
L	50
C	100
D	500
M	1000

Examples

1 Change the following into Roman numerals:

a) 46   **b)** 121   *a) 46 = XLVI   b) 121 = CXXI*

2 Change the following Roman numerals into our numbers:

a) LXXVII   **b)** MCMXCIX   *a) LXXVII = 77   b) MCMXCIX = 1999*

Key fact

You need to remember the rules about the position of a figure. If it is placed to the left of a figure of higher value, you subtract.

Language

Some of the Roman numerals use the 1st letter of a word – for example C stands for century, i.e. 100.

On track

1 Convert the following Roman numerals into our numbers.

   a) XXII *22*   **b)** XVI *16*   **c)** LIV *54*   **d** DXXXIX *539*

2 Convert the following numbers into Roman numerals.

   a) 232   **b)** 413   **c)** 155   **d)** 989

   CCXXXII   *CDXIII*   *CLV*   *CMLXXXIX*

Aiming higher

1 Change these years to Roman numerals.

   a) 1953   **b)** 939   **c)** 1588   **d)** 1945

   MCMLIII   *CMXXXIX*   *MDLXXXVIII*   *MCMXLV*

2 Change these Roman numerals into years.

   a) MLXVI   **b)** MDLIX   **c)** MDCLXV   **d)** MMXIIII

   1066   *1559*   *1665*   *2014*

Using and applying

1 From Nottingham to Leicester is about 28 miles. Write this distance in Roman numerals.

2 A milestone at the side of the road states: LXIV miles to Beeton. How far is this using our numbers?

4 Volume

What will you learn?

I need to know how to:

● recognise and estimate volume, e.g. using 1 cm blocks to build cubes and cuboids.

I need to be able to:

● multiply whole numbers together.

Example

Find the volume of this cuboid.

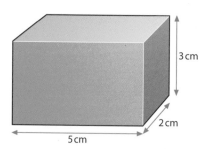

Five 1 cm blocks will fit in a row along the length. There will be two rows covering the base, and because the cuboid is 3 cm high there will be three levels or layers of the two rows.

There are $5 \times 2 \times 3 = 30$ lots of 1 cm cubes.

The volume is 30 cubic centimetres or 30 cm³.

Key fact

Volume is found by multiplying together the number of 1 cm cubes that fit in a row along the length by the number of rows that fit along the width and by number of rows that fit in the depth or height.

Language

Volume   of a solid or shape is the amount of space it fills or occupies.

A **cuboid** is a solid with six faces that are rectangles. The opposite sides are exactly the same. Each edge is perpendicular to the edges that are joined to it.

On track

1 How many small cubes make up each of these cuboids?

a)

18

b)

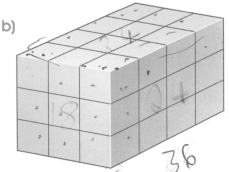

36

2 a) How many 1 cm cubes will be needed to form a layer covering the base of each of these shapes?

i)

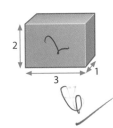

ii)

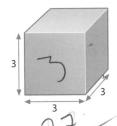

27

iii)

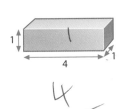

4

b) How many layers will there be in each shape?

c) What is the volume of each shape?

6 cm³   27 cm³   4 cm³

Aiming higher

1 How many 1 cm cubes will fit into a hollow cube if the sides of the cube are 5 cm?

2 It takes 24 1 cm cubes to fill a cuboid exactly. Find possible answers for the number of cubes that will make a row across the length, for the number of rows to cover the base in a layer and the number of layers that will be needed.
(There are 6 possible combinations – try to find them all.)

Using and applying

1 A cube has a volume of 125 cm³. What are the lengths of its sides?

2 A box has a length of 4 cm, a width of 3 cm and a height of 2 cm. Work out its volume.

5 Place value, rounding and ordering numbers

What will you learn?

How to:

- read, write, order and compare numbers to at least 1 000 000 and know the value of each digit

- round any number up to 1 000 000 to the nearest 10, 100, 1000, 10 000 and 100 000

- read, write, order and compare numbers with up to 3 decimal places

- round decimal numbers with two decimal places to the nearest whole number and to one decimal place.

With whole numbers up to 1000 and in decimals with up to 2 decimal places

I need to be able to:

- understand what each digit represents

- partition, round and order these numbers

- put these numbers in size order.

Examples

1 What is the **value** of the 7 in 64 105.73?

50 700 46 can be written as 5 000 000 + 70 000 + 40 + 6. Write 64 105.73 in the same way.

You may find it helpful to put the number into columns as shown.

Ten thousands	Thousands	Hundreds	Tens	Units		tenths	hundredths
6	4	1	0	5		7	3

The 7 is in the tenths column and so it represents seven tenths or 0.7.

60 000 + 4000 + 100 + 5 + 0.7 + 0.03.

Round 17.46 and 19.58 to the nearest whole number.

Look at the decimal part of each number. In 17.46 the 46 is less than 50, i.e. less than half, so round down to 17. But in 19.58 the 58 is more than 50 so round up to 20.

3 Put these numbers in order of size, largest first:

0.618   0.8   0.073   0.736   0.592

First, write the numbers
In the place value table:

Next, sort them into order starting with the furthest left column used and the largest digit in this column:

U	.	$\frac{1}{10}$	$\frac{1}{100}$	$\frac{1}{1000}$
0	.	6	1	8
0	.	8		
0	.	0	7	3
0	.	7	3	6
0	.	5	9	2

U	.	$\frac{1}{10}$	$\frac{1}{100}$	$\frac{1}{1000}$
0	.	8		
0	.	7	3	6
0	.	6	1	8
0	.	5	9	2
0	.	0	7	3

The largest number is 0.8.

Hint: A common mistake is to assume that, for example, 0.736 is bigger than 0.8 because it has three figures in it.

4 Round 1356 to the nearest a) 10 b) 100.

a)   1356 is between 1350 and 1360.

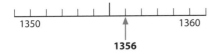

So 1356 will be rounded up to 1360 because it is nearer to 1360 than 1350.

b)   1356 is between 1300 and 1400.

So 1356 will be rounded up to 1400 because it is nearer to 1400 than 1300

5 Round:

a)   0.7 to the nearest whole number

b)   0.75 to one decimal place

c)   2.34 to the nearest whole number

d)   2.34 to one decimal place.

6 a)

Use the number line to help:
0.7 is nearer to 1.0 than to zero.
So 0.7 rounds up to 1.

b)

Use the number line to help:
0.75 is half way between 0.7 and 0.8.
The rule is that when a number if exactly half way between 2 numbers i.e. the last digit is 5, then round up. 0.75 rounds up to 0.8.

c) To the nearest whole number, 2.34 rounds down to 2 because it is nearer to 2 than it is to 3. Look at the number line below.

2.0 2.1 2.2 2.3 2.4 2.5 2.6 2.7 2.8 2.9 3.0

d) To one decimal place, 2.34 rounds down to 2.3. Look at the number line in part c).

Key facts

The decimal point marks the separation between whole numbers and decimals. Remember to use a number line – look at the examples above. Any number in the middle or to the right of the middle rounds up. So, with a number line from 0 to 10, 5 or a number greater than 5 will round up to 10. Any number less than 5 rounds down to zero.

0   1   2   3   4   5   6   7   8   9   10

Language

Value   the value of a digit is given by its position – how many hundreds or tenths, etc. it represents

Remember the names of large numbers:

Million   1 million is 1 000 000 and, for example, 6 million is 6 000 000

Hundred thousand   1 hundred thousand is 100 000, 7 hundred thousand is 700 000

Decimal place   is used with a number to show how many figures after the decimal point there are. So 2.34 has 2 decimal places; 14.567 has 3 decimal places

On track

1 Put these numbers in order, smallest first.

3.66   9   7.25   5.63   6.2   3.83   2.99

2 What do the digits   a) 2   b) 7   c) 3   represent in the number 2.37?

3 What number should be written in each box in these questions?

a)   275 = 200 + [20] + 5

b)   600 + [50] + 9 = 659

c)   3012 = [3000] + 10 + 2

d)   9[7]4 = 900 + 70 + 4

e)   10[4]7 = 1000 + 40 + 7

f)   [9]07 = 900 + 7

4 a)   Write these numbers to the nearest 10.

   i) 651   **ii)** 655   **iii)** 529   **iv)** 495   **v)** 997

b) Write these numbers to the nearest 100.

i) 8632   ii) 5614   iii) 9901   iv) 9960   v) 1094

c) Write these numbers to the nearest 1000.

i) 8632   ii) 5614   iii) 9901   iv) 9960   v) 1094

Aiming higher

1 Write the value of the 5 in 21.57 as a fraction and then as a decimal.

2 Write these numbers using whole numbers and decimals (not fractions).

a) six thousand and twelve
b) nine-tenths
c) one and three-tenths
d) six, one-tenth and seven hundredths

3 Write these numbers in figures:

a) Six thousand and twenty-five   b) Eight hundred and ten

4 Write these numbers in words:

a) 403   b) 1076   c) 1007   d) 5391

5 a) Put these numbers in order of size, smallest first.

0.667   0.66   0.088   0.625

b) What is the difference between the largest and smallest number?

Using and applying

1 This table shows the population of some cities In America in 2010. The numbers have been rounded to the nearest thousand.

Atlanta	420 000	Miami	399 000
Baltimore	621 000	Dallas	1 198 000
Chicago	2 696 000	New York	8 175 000
Cleveland	397 000	Philadelphia	1 526 000
Detroit	714 000	Phoenix	1 446 000
Houston	2 099 000	Washington	602 000
Los Angeles	3 793 000	Las Vegas	584 000

a) Which cities have a smaller population than Baltimore?

b) What is the population of Chicago to the nearest million?

c) The population of Birmingham, England, in 2010 was around 1 036 900. Which of the American cities in the list was closest in population to Birmingham?

6 Fractions

What will you learn?

How to:

- compare and order fractions whose denominators are all multiples of the same number
- recognise mixed numbers and improper fractions and convert from one to another.

I need to be able to:

- find equivalent fractions
- simplify fractions
- multiply and divide numbers by, for example, 2, 3, 4 5.

Examples

1 Write these fractions in order, smallest first. $\dfrac{3}{4}$ $\dfrac{4}{5}$ $\dfrac{7}{10}$ $\dfrac{13}{20}$

You can make and then compare equivalent fractions by finding a common denominator: a number that all the denominators (4, 5, 10 and 20) divide into exactly. The smallest common denominator is 20.

Fractions $\dfrac{3}{4}$ $\dfrac{4}{5}$ $\dfrac{7}{10}$ $\dfrac{13}{20}$

Equivalent fractions $\dfrac{15}{20}$ $\dfrac{16}{20}$ $\dfrac{14}{20}$ $\dfrac{13}{20}$

So the answer is: $\dfrac{13}{20}$ $\dfrac{7}{10}$ $\dfrac{3}{4}$ $\dfrac{4}{5}$

You can make and then compare equivalent fractions using decimals.

Using decimals: $\dfrac{7}{10} = 0.7$ $\dfrac{4}{5} = 0.8$ $\dfrac{3}{4} = 0.75$ $\dfrac{13}{20} = 0.65$

So the answer is: $\dfrac{13}{20}$ $\dfrac{7}{10}$ $\dfrac{3}{4}$ $\dfrac{4}{5}$

2 Complete the following:

a) $\dfrac{2}{5} = \dfrac{\square}{15}$

$\dfrac{2}{5} = \dfrac{6}{15}$ The denominator, 5, has been multiplied by 3 so multiplying the numerator by 3 gives $2 \times 3 = 6$.

b) $\dfrac{6}{14} = \dfrac{3}{\square}$

$\dfrac{6}{14} = \dfrac{3}{7}$ *The numerator, 6, has been divided by 2 so dividing the denominator by 2 gives $14 \div 2 = 7$.*

3 Change these mixed numbers into improper fractions:

a) $1\dfrac{1}{3}$ **b)** $2\dfrac{3}{4}$ **c)** $5\dfrac{1}{2}$

a) $1\dfrac{1}{3}$ *In full the working is: the denominator of the fraction is 3 – so we are working in thirds. There are three thirds in 1 and there is 1 third left over so there are 4 thirds altogether. The answer is $\dfrac{4}{3}$. The quick way is to multiply the whole number by the denominator, this tells you how many thirds there are in the whole number and then add the numerator – so $1 \times 3 = 3$.*

$3 + 1 = 4$ *so the improper fraction is $\dfrac{4}{3}$.*

It may be easier to look at a diagram:

3 squares shaded making a whole

1 square shaded from the next 'whole' making a whole making 4 squares shaded in total so $\dfrac{4}{3}$

b) $2\dfrac{3}{4}$ *Multiply the whole number by the denominator: $2 \times 4 = 8$. Then add the numerator. $8 + 3 = 11$ so the answer is $\dfrac{11}{4}$.*

c) $5\dfrac{1}{2}$ *Multiply the whole number by the denominator – $5 \times 2 = 10$. Add the numerator. $10 + 1 = 11$ so the answer is $\dfrac{11}{2}$.*

4 Change these improper fractions to mixed numbers:

a) $\dfrac{7}{2}$ **b)** $\dfrac{5}{4}$ **c)** $\dfrac{9}{5}$

a) $\dfrac{7}{2}$ *Divide the denominator into the numerator. $7 \div 2 = 3$ remainder 1. In other words, there are 3 wholes and a remainder of $\dfrac{1}{2}$ so the answer is $3\dfrac{1}{2}$.*

b) $\dfrac{5}{4}$ *Divide 4 into 5. $5 \div 4 = 1$, remainder $\dfrac{1}{4}$ so the answer is $1\dfrac{1}{4}$.*

c) $\dfrac{5}{4}$ *Divide 9 into 5. $9 \div 5 = 1$, remainder $\dfrac{4}{5}$ so the answer is $1\dfrac{4}{5}$.*

Key facts

Equivalent fractions have the same value.
To compare fractions use equivalent fractions with a common denominator or convert them into decimals.
A fraction is in its lowest terms when there is no equivalent fraction with a smaller denominator.

Language

Numerator   the top number of a fraction
Denominator   the bottom number of a fraction
Equivalent   means 'the same as'
Simplify   means to find an equivalent fraction with the smallest denominator possible
Proper fraction   one where the numerator is less than the denominator
Improper fraction   one where the numerator is greater than the denominator. Another name for it is a 'top heavy' fraction

On track

1   Here is a chocolate bar.

Bill eats 5 pieces and Alison eats 3 pieces.
What fraction of the chocolate bar remains?

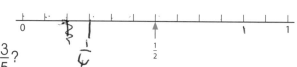

2   Mark $\frac{1}{4}$ and $\frac{5}{6}$ on this number line.

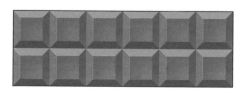

3   Which of these fractions is the same as $\frac{3}{5}$?

$\frac{7}{9}$ $\boxed{\frac{6}{10}}$ $\frac{8}{12}$ $\boxed{\frac{9}{15}}$ $\boxed{\frac{18}{30}}$ $\boxed{\frac{30}{50}}$

4   Change these improper fractions to mixed numbers.

a) $\frac{11}{5}$ $2\frac{1}{5}$ b) $\frac{10}{7}$ $1\frac{3}{7}$ c) $\frac{8}{3}$ $2\frac{2}{3}$ d) $\frac{9}{4}$ $2\frac{1}{4}$

5   Change these mixed numbers to improper fractions.

a) $1\frac{5}{6}$ $\frac{11}{6}$ b) $2\frac{3}{8}$ $\frac{19}{8}$ c) $1\frac{3}{5}$ $\frac{8}{5}$ d) $3\frac{1}{4}$ $\frac{13}{4}$

6   Compare these fractions. Write down two that are greater than $\frac{1}{2}$.

$\frac{3}{20}$ $\boxed{\frac{7}{10}}$ $\frac{4}{8}$ $\boxed{\frac{10}{15}}$ $\frac{2}{5}$

Aiming higher

1 What is the missing number? How do you know?

$$\frac{3}{10} = \frac{\boxed{9}}{30}$$

2 How could you show that $\frac{3}{12}$ is equivalent to $\frac{1}{4}$?

3 Here are two number cards. One of the cards is 12.
The two number cards can make a fraction equivalent to a quarter.
What two values could the second card be?

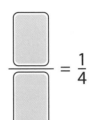

4 Amy has these number cards.

a) List all the fractions she can make by choosing pairs of cards.

b) Write your fractions as proper fractions or mixed numbers.

c) Write your fractions in order of size, smallest first.

5 Which of these fractions has a different value from the others?

$$\frac{4}{6} \qquad \frac{9}{14} \qquad \frac{40}{60} \qquad \frac{8}{12} \qquad \frac{6}{9} \qquad \frac{2}{3}$$

Using and applying

1 Which of the following fractions is closest to $\frac{1}{2}$?

$$\frac{7}{16} \qquad \frac{3}{24} \qquad \frac{1}{3} \qquad \boxed{\frac{3}{8}} \qquad \frac{3}{4}$$

How can you tell?

2 Ages can be written as mixed numbers.
For example, a boy who is 8 years and 5 months would write his age as $8\frac{5}{12}$.

Complete this table:

Years and months		Months	Mixed number
5	7	67	$5\frac{5}{12}$
9	3	111	$9\frac{3}{12}$
			$10\frac{4}{12}$
		89	

How else could you write **a)** the fraction $9\frac{3}{12}$ and **b)** the fraction $10\frac{4}{12}$?

7 Calculating with fractions

What will you learn?

How to:

- add and subtract fractions with the same denominator and related fractions
- multiply proper fractions and mixed numbers by whole numbers supported by materials and diagrams
- write mathematical statements >1 as a mixed number, e.g. $\frac{2}{5} + \frac{4}{5} = \frac{6}{5} = 1\frac{1}{5}$

I need to know how to:

- find equivalent fractions
- simplify fractions
- change mixed numbers into fractions.

Examples

1 Calculate:

    a) $\frac{2}{5} + \frac{1}{5}$ **b)** $\frac{2}{3} - \frac{1}{5}$ **c)** $\frac{1}{8} \times 5$ **d)** $3 \times \frac{1}{2}$ **e)** $1\frac{2}{3} \times 3$ **f)** $5 \times 3\frac{1}{4}$

   a) $\frac{2}{5} + \frac{1}{5}$ *The denominators are the same, so add the numerators:*

     $\frac{2}{5} + \frac{1}{5} = \frac{3}{5}$

   b) $\frac{2}{3} - \frac{1}{5}$ *The denominators are different, so the fractions must be changed*
                 into equivalent fractions with the same denominators:

     $\frac{2}{3} - \frac{1}{5} = \frac{10}{15} - \frac{3}{15}$

          $= \frac{7}{15}$

   c) $\frac{1}{8} \times 5$ *In this diagram, $\frac{1}{8}$ is* [diagram] *shaded.*

           In this diagram, five times as much is shaded.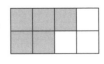
           This shows that $\frac{1}{8} \times 5 = \frac{5}{8}$

           To multiply a proper fraction by an integer, just multiply the
           numerator by the integer

d) $3 \times \dfrac{1}{2}$ This diagram shows $\dfrac{1}{2}$ a pizza.

This diagram shows 3 half-pizzas.
This can be written as $\dfrac{3}{2}$.

You can put two of the halves
together to make a whole pizza.

This shows that $3 \times \dfrac{1}{2} = \dfrac{3}{2} = 1 \text{ whole} + \dfrac{1}{2} = 1\dfrac{1}{2}$

e) $1\dfrac{2}{3} \times 3$ The simplest way is to change the mixed number into an improper fraction:

$$1\dfrac{2}{3} \times 3 = \dfrac{5}{3} \times 3$$

Then multiply the numerator by the whole number: $5 \times 3 = 15$

$$= \dfrac{15}{3} = 5$$

f) $5 \times 3\dfrac{1}{4}$ In the same way, this becomes

$$5 \times 3\dfrac{1}{4} = 5 \times \dfrac{13}{4}$$
$$= \dfrac{65}{4}$$
$$= 16\dfrac{1}{4}$$

2 Find:

a) $\dfrac{1}{2}$ of £30   **b)** $\dfrac{3}{4}$ of 48 metres

a) Find $\dfrac{1}{2} \times 30 = 15$ so the answer is £15

b) First find of $\dfrac{1}{4}$ of $48 = 12$. Then multiply this answer by $3 = 36$.
   So the answer is 36 metres.

3 Calculate:

a) $1\dfrac{3}{5} + \dfrac{4}{5}$ **b)** $1\dfrac{5}{8} - \dfrac{7}{8}$ **c)** $1\dfrac{3}{4} + 1\dfrac{1}{4}$ **d)** $2\dfrac{3}{7} - 1\dfrac{4}{7}$ **e)** $3\dfrac{3}{4} + 2\dfrac{3}{5}$

a) $1\dfrac{3}{5} + \dfrac{4}{5} = \dfrac{8}{5} + \dfrac{4}{5} = \dfrac{12}{5} = 2\dfrac{2}{5}$

Change the mixed number into an improper fraction. Add the numerators and
then change back into a mixed number by dividing the numerator, 12, by 5.

b) $1\frac{5}{8} - \frac{7}{8} = \frac{13}{8} - \frac{7}{8} = \frac{6}{8} = \frac{3}{4}$

Change the mixed number into an improper fraction. Subtract the numerators and then in this case simplify the fraction.

c) $1\frac{3}{4} + 1\frac{1}{4} = \frac{7}{4} + \frac{5}{4} = \frac{12}{4} = 3$

Change the mixed numbers into improper fractions. Add the numerators and then simplify by dividing the numerator, 12, by 4.

d) $2\frac{3}{7} - 1\frac{4}{7} = \frac{17}{7} - \frac{11}{7} = \frac{6}{7}$

Change the mixed numbers into improper fractions before subtracting the denominators.

e) $3\frac{3}{4} + 2\frac{3}{5} = \frac{15}{4} + \frac{13}{5} = \frac{75}{20} + \frac{52}{20} = \frac{127}{20} = 6\frac{7}{20}$

Change the mixed numbers into improper fractions. Then, as the denominators are different, the common denominator is 20, so change into equivalent fractions and add.

Key fact

In order to add or subtract fractions you must make sure the fractions have the same denominators – in other words, you need to add or subtract parts of the same thing. However, when multiplying, make sure you change mixed numbers into improper fractions before multiplying by the whole number.

Language

Numerator   the top number of a fraction

Denominator   the bottom number of a fraction

Mixed number   a whole number and a fraction. $5\frac{1}{4}$ is a mixed number

Improper fractions   a fraction where the numerator is larger than the denominator

On track

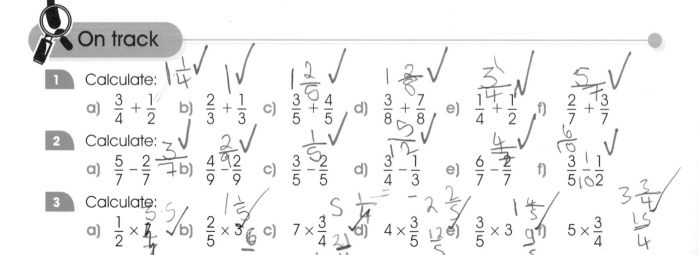

1 Calculate:

a) $\frac{3}{4} + \frac{1}{2}$ b) $\frac{2}{3} + \frac{1}{3}$ c) $\frac{3}{5} + \frac{4}{5}$ d) $\frac{3}{8} + \frac{7}{8}$ e) $\frac{1}{4} + \frac{1}{2}$ f) $\frac{2}{7} + \frac{3}{7}$

2 Calculate:

a) $\frac{5}{7} - \frac{2}{7}$ b) $\frac{4}{9} - \frac{2}{9}$ c) $\frac{3}{5} - \frac{2}{5}$ d) $\frac{3}{4} - \frac{1}{3}$ e) $\frac{6}{7} - \frac{2}{7}$ f) $\frac{3}{5} - \frac{1}{2}$

3 Calculate:

a) $\frac{1}{2} \times \frac{7}{1}$ b) $\frac{2}{5} \times 3$ c) $7 \times \frac{3}{4}$ d) $4 \times \frac{3}{5}$ e) $\frac{3}{5} \times 3$ f) $5 \times \frac{3}{4}$

$^a \dfrac{6}{2} = 3$ ✓ $^b \dfrac{42}{5} = 8\frac{2}{5}$ ✓ $^c \dfrac{45}{4} = 11\frac{1}{4}$

4 Calculate:

a) $2 \times 1\frac{1}{2}$ b) $4\frac{1}{5} \times 2$ c) $5 \times 2\frac{1}{4}$ d) $5\frac{3}{8} \times 5$ e) $\frac{3}{4} \times 9$ f) $5 \times \frac{3}{8}$

5 Calculate:

a) $\frac{3}{4}$ of 24 cm   b) $\frac{2}{3}$ of 60 metres   c) $\frac{1}{4}$ of £120   d) $\frac{1}{5}$ of 40 litres

6 Calculate:

a) $2\frac{3}{4} + 3\frac{3}{4}$ b) $4\frac{1}{6} - 2\frac{5}{6}$ c) $3\frac{1}{4} + 3\frac{1}{8}$ d) $5\frac{1}{3} - 3\frac{2}{5}$

Aiming higher

1 Here are four fraction cards.

$\boxed{\frac{1}{4}}$ $\boxed{\frac{1}{3}}$ $\boxed{\frac{3}{4}}$ $\boxed{\frac{2}{3}}$

Put the cards into two piles which have the same total.

2 Calculate the fraction that is $\frac{1}{7}$ less than $\frac{1}{4}$.

3 Find the missing numbers in this calculation.

$$\dfrac{\square}{5} + \dfrac{1}{\square} + \dfrac{\square}{5} = 1$$

4 Complete this multiplication grid.

×		$\frac{3}{5}$
4	$\frac{8}{3}$	
	$\frac{6}{3}$ (= 2)	$\frac{9}{5}$

Using and applying

1 Fred cuts 4 pieces of string each $\frac{3}{5}$ metre long. How much string did he use?

2 A washing machine is normally for sale at £400.

In a sale this price is reduced by a fifth.

a) What is the reduction?   b) What is the new price?

$\dfrac{9}{12} - \dfrac{4}{12}$

$\dfrac{3}{4} = \dfrac{9}{12}$ $\dfrac{1}{3} = \dfrac{4}{12}$

8 Fractions and decimals

What will you learn?

How to:

- read and write decimal numbers as fractions
- recognise and use thousandths and relate them to tenths, hundredths and decimal equivalents.

I need to be able to:

- recognise that with decimal numbers the value of each digit is given by its position or place.

Examples

1 This table shows the place value of some numbers:

Number	Hundreds	Tens	Units	.	Tenths $\frac{1}{10}$	Hundredths $\frac{1}{100}$	Thousandths $\frac{1}{1000}$
145.3	1	4	5	.	3		
74.89		7	4	.	8	9	
12.356		1	2	.	3	5	6
0.674			0	.	6	7	4

145.3 can be written as $145\frac{3}{10}$

12.356 Can be written as $12\frac{3}{10} + \frac{5}{100} + \frac{6}{1000} = 12\frac{356}{1000}$.

(This can be simplified to $12\frac{178}{500} = 12\frac{89}{250}$ by dividing the numerator and denominator of the fraction by 2 and then by 2 again.)

Now write 74.89 and 0.674 as fractions.

Use the table to help: $74.89 = 74 + \frac{8}{10} + \frac{9}{100} = 74\frac{89}{100}$

$$0.674 = 0 + \frac{6}{10} + \frac{7}{100} + \frac{4}{1000} = \frac{674}{1000}$$

2 Change **a)** $1\frac{4}{10}$ **b)** $\frac{74}{100}$ **c)** $4\frac{64}{1000}$ into decimals. *a) 1.4   b) 0.74   c) 4.064*

Use the table to help.

Key fact

The decimal point marks the separation between whole numbers and decimals.

Language

Value   the value of a digit is given by its position – how many hundreds or tenths, etc. it represents

> **tenths (t)**   are $\frac{1}{10}$ of one unit
>
> **hundredths (h)**   are $\frac{1}{100}$ of one unit
>
> **thousandths (th)**   are $\frac{1}{1000}$ of one unit
>
> **to two decimal places**   means 'to the nearest hundredth'

Remember, the decimal fraction number names below zero are the same as the names above the units with 'th' added, starting with tenths.

On track

1. Write 37 plus 3 hundredths plus 7 thousandths as a decimal.

2. Write the total of this calculation using decimals:
   $$6 + \frac{3}{10} + \frac{7}{100} =$$

3. Write a number in the box to make this correct:
   $$7.35 = 7 + 0.3 + \boxed{}$$

4. Change into fractions:
   a) 4.3   b) 23.56   c) 7.567

Aiming higher

1. Write these numbers using whole numbers and decimals, not fractions.
   a) six thousand and twelve   b) nine-tenths
   c) one and three-tenths   d) six, one-tenth and seven-hundredths

2. Copy and complete these expressions.
   a) $\frac{1}{10} + \frac{4}{10} = 0.1 + 0.\boxed{} = \boxed{}$ b) $\frac{3}{10} + \frac{8}{10} = \frac{\boxed{}}{10} = 1.\boxed{}$

   c) $\frac{4}{10} + \frac{3}{100} = 0.\boxed{}$

3 Copy and complete these expressions.

a) $35.7 = 30 + \boxed{} + \dfrac{\boxed{}}{10}$

b) $75.345 = 70 + 5 + \dfrac{\boxed{}}{10} + \dfrac{4}{\boxed{}} + \dfrac{5}{\boxed{}}$

4 This grid has 10 squares. 5 of them are shaded.

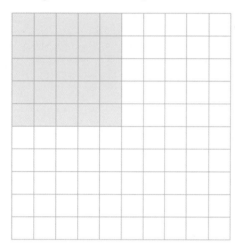 You can see that $\dfrac{5}{10} = \dfrac{1}{2} = 0.5$

This grid has 100 squares. 25 are shaded.

You can see that $\dfrac{25}{100} = \dfrac{1}{4} = 0.25$

Using squared paper if you need to, copy and complete this table:

Fraction	$\dfrac{1}{2}$	$\dfrac{1}{4}$			$\dfrac{2}{5}$		$\dfrac{4}{5}$
Decimal	0.5	0.25	0.75	0.2		0.6	

 Using and applying

1 Write a decimal that contains seven units and five hundredths.

2 Write a number that is bigger than 0.4 but smaller than 0.5.

3 Write the following as decimals:

a) six and one tenth

b) six hundredths

c) sixty hundredths

d) one and one hundredth

4 Write down two numbers that add to 8 and differ by 1.

9 Understanding percentages

What will you learn?

How to:

● recognise the % symbol and understand that per cent relates to number of parts per hundred

● write percentages as fractions with denominator 100 and as decimal fractions.

I need to be able to:

● know how to multiply and divide by 10

● recognise the place value in decimals.

Examples

1 Shade 10% of this grid.

There are 100 squares. Per cent means 'out of 100' so 10% is 10 out of 100, so 10 squares are shaded. 10% can be written as $\frac{10}{100} = \frac{1}{10}$.

2 Write these percentages as simplified fractions.

50%   6%   20%   30%

$50\% = \frac{50}{100} = \frac{1}{2}$ $6\% = \frac{6}{100} = \frac{3}{50}$ $20\% = \frac{20}{100} = \frac{1}{5}$ $30\% = \frac{30}{100} = \frac{3}{10}$

3 Change these fractions and decimals to percentages

a) $\frac{2}{5}$ **b)** $\frac{8}{25}$ **c)** 0.37   **d)** 0.07

a) $\frac{2}{5}$ needs to become hundredths; percentages are fractions using hundredths.

$\frac{2}{5} = \frac{\ }{100}$ (5 has been multiplied by 20 to give 100, so 2 must be multiplied by the same number.)

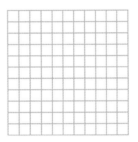

$\frac{2 \times 20}{5 \times 20} = \frac{40}{100}$

$\frac{40}{100} = 40\%$

b) $\frac{8}{25}$ needs to become hundredths; percentages are fractions using hundredths.

$\frac{8}{25} = \frac{\ }{100}$ (25 has been multiplied by 4 to give 100, so 8 must be multiplied by the same number.)

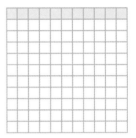

$\frac{8 \times 4}{25 \times 4} = \frac{32}{100}$

$\frac{32}{100} = 32\%$

c) 0.37 becomes 0.37 × 100 = 37   So 0.37 as a percentage is 37%

d) 0.07 becomes 0.07 × 100 = 7   So 0.07 as a percentage is 7%

Key fact

Fractions are used to describe parts of a whole.

Percentages are fractions with denominators of 100, for example 5% represents $\frac{5}{100}$, 37% represents $\frac{37}{100}$, 88% represents $\frac{88}{100}$. It is often useful to remember that 1% = $\frac{1}{100}$ and use this fact to work out other percentages as fractions.

Language

Percentage means 'per cent' or 'per hundred' – think about 'century' meaning 100 years, or 100 runs in cricket

On track

1 a) Copy and shade 20% of this 8 × 5 grid.

b) Copy and shade 35% of this 10 × 10 grid.

$$\frac{35}{50} \qquad \frac{70}{100}$$

2 What is $\frac{45}{100}$ as a percentage? 0.45

3 What percentage of the bar is shaded?

$\frac{6}{10}$ 60%

4 A test has 50 marks. Rory gets 35 marks. What is his percentage score? 70%

5 What percentage of this shape is shaded?

a) ☐ 50%   b) ■ 20%   c) ☐ 30%

d) In another pattern using grey, black and white squares, 20% are grey, 40% are black. What percentage is white?

6 Change these decimals into percentages:

16:5   132%

a) 0.62 62%   b) 0.56 56%   c) 0.04 4%   d) 0.165   e) 1.32

7 Change these decimals into percentages:

a) $\frac{7}{10}$ 70%   b) $\frac{3}{5}$ 60%   c) $\frac{7}{20}$ 35%   d) $\frac{10}{25}$ 40%   e) $\frac{17}{50}$ 34%

Aiming higher

1 Write these percentages as fractions:

a) 40% $\frac{40}{100}$ b) 33% $\frac{33}{100}$ c) 70% $\frac{70}{100}$ d) 24% $\frac{24}{100}$ e) 12% $\frac{12}{100}$

2 Write these fractions as percentages:

a) $\frac{30}{100}$ 30%   b) $\frac{25}{100}$ 25%   c) $\frac{1}{2}$ 50%   d) $\frac{1}{4}$ 25%   e) $\frac{3}{4}$ 75%

3 45% of a class of children are boys. What percentage are girls? 55

4 Put these numbers in order, smallest first:

0.44   45% $\frac{14}{100}$ $\frac{34}{10}$

5 a) Write a **percentage** that is **greater than** $\frac{8}{10}$ and **less than** $\frac{90}{100}$. 85%

   b) Write a **decimal** that is **greater than** 25% and **less than** 50%. ·45

   c) Write a **decimal** that is **greater than** $\frac{1}{2}$ and **less than** 75%. ·70

Using and applying

1 Copy and complete this table.

Fractions	Decimals	Percentage
$\frac{1}{4}$	0·25	25%
$\frac{5}{100}$	0.5	50%
$\frac{7}{10}$	0·7	70%

2 Match the decimals in row **A** with the percentages in row **B**.

A	0.05	0.7	0.5	0.75	1.0	0.075	0.45
B	100%	5%	70%	75%	50%	45%	7.5%

3 Some interesting facts:

Rewrite the underlined words using percentages.

a) About <u>three fifths</u> of the world's population lives in Asia. 60%

b) <u>One in twenty</u> males are colour-blind. 5%

c) About <u>one eighth</u> of an iceberg shows above water.

4 A, E, I, O, U are vowels.

a) What fraction of the letters in your name are vowels? $\frac{3}{5}$

b) What percentage of the letters in your name are vowels? 60%

c) Try to find 2 words which both have 20% of their letters as vowels.

10 Multiplying and dividing by 10, 100, 1000

What will you learn?

How to:

● multiply and divide whole numbers and those involving decimals by 10, 100, and 1000.

I need to be able to:

● recognise that with decimal numbers the value of each digit is given by its position or place

● use a calculator efficiently.

Examples

1 Find the missing numbers without using a calculator.

$39 \times ? = 390 \qquad 6000 \div ? = 60$

● *10 – the 3 in the tens column has moved into the hundreds column.*

● *100 – the 6 in the thousands column has moved into the tens column.*

2 Calculate: **a)** 4.62×100 **b)** $37.46 \div 100$ **c)** 243.6×1000

You may find it helpful to look at the table in the Key facts.

a) *Multiplying 4.62 by 100 involves moving each digit 2 columns to the left:*

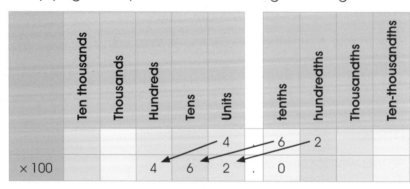

b) Dividing 37.46 by 100 involves moving each digit 2 columns to the right.
Remember to put a 0 (zero) in the units column to show that there are no units.

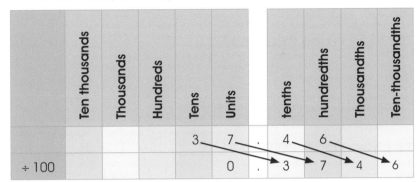

	Ten thousands	Thousands	Hundreds	Tens	Units		tenths	hundredths	Thousandths	Ten-thousandths
				3	7 .		4	6		
÷ 100				0	.		3	7	4	6

c) Multiplying 243.6 by 1000 involves moving each digit 3 columns to the left.
Remember to put a zero in the tens column and the units column to show that
there are no numbers there, otherwise the answer would be 2436.0.

	Hundred thousands	Ten thousands	Thousands	Hundreds	Tens	Units		tenths
					2	4	3 .	6
× 1000	2	4	3	6	0	0	.	

Key facts

	Ten thousands	Thousands	Hundreds	Tens	Units		tenths	hundredths	Thousandths	Ten-thousandths
× 10				6	8 .		1	2		
× 100		6	8	1	2 .		0			
× 1000	6	8	1	2	0					
				6	8 .		1	2		
÷ 10					6 .		8	1	2	
÷ 100					0 .		6	8	1	2

Multiplying by 10 moves digits one column to the left, multiplying by 100 moves them 2 columns to the left, multiplying by 1000 moves them 3 places to the left. Dividing by 10 moves digits one column to the right, dividing by 100 moves them two columns to the right and so on.

Language

Tenths (t) $\frac{1}{10}$ of a unit

Hundredths (h) $\frac{1}{100}$ of a unit

On track

1. How many tens are there in one thousand? 100(

2. Divide 8400 by 100. 84

3. Write in the missing number: 5600 ÷ 56 = 100

4. Write what the four missing digits could be: ☐☐☐ ÷ 10 = 3☐.☐

5. Divide 101.1 by 10.

6. Calculate:

   a) 13.4×100 b) 746.42×1000 c) $46.9 \div 100$ d) $999.99 \div 1000$

7. Find the missing numbers.

   a) $56 \times \boxed{100} = 5600$ b) $73.8 \div \boxed{} = 7.38$

   c) $34.05 \times \boxed{100} = 3405$ d) $802 \div \boxed{} = 0.802$

   e) $0.7 \times \boxed{} = 700$ f) $9.1 \div \boxed{} = 0.091$

   g) $583 \times \boxed{} = 58300$ h) $67080 \div = 6708$

Aiming higher

1. Find the missing numbers.

   a) $50 = 5 \times \boxed{}$ b) $700 = 7 \times \boxed{}$

   c) $8000 = 8 \times \boxed{}$ d) $400 = 40 \times \boxed{}$

2. Find the missing numbers.

   a) Multiplying a number by 10 and then multiplying the answer by 10 again is the same as multiplying by ☐.

   b) Multiplying a number by 100 and then multiplying the answer by 10 again is the same as multiplying by ☐.

3. Calculate:

   a) 60×40 b) 300×30 c) 70×20 d) 90×600

   e) 500×7 f) 9×90 g) 500×20 h) 100×100

Using and applying

1 I divide a number by 10, and then again by 10. The answer is 0.8.
What number did I start with? How can you check?

2 What number is ten times as big as 0.03? How do you know?

3 What numbers should you write in the boxes?

a) $6800 \div 6800 = \boxed{0}$

b) $6800 \div 680 = \boxed{}$

c) $6800 \div 68 = \boxed{}$

4 A length of rope is 294 cm long. It is cut into ten equal pieces.
How long is each piece?

(not to scale)

5 A torch battery will last 4.5×1000 seconds.

a) How many seconds is this?

b) Is this more or less than 5000 seconds?

11 Multiplication and division

What will you learn?

How to:

- multiply numbers up to 4-digits by a 1- or 2- digit number using an efficient written method, including long multiplication for two-digit numbers

- divide numbers up to 4 digits by a 1-digit number using the efficient written method of short division and interpret remainders appropriately for the context

- solve problems involving multiplication and division including scaling by simple fractions and problems involving simple rates

- solve word problems involving multiplication and division.

I need to know:

- how to estimate the answers to questions.

Examples

1 Work out 13×7.

You will know that there are three ways of doing this:

The grid method

$\times$	7
10	70
3	21
	91

$70 + 21 = 91$

The expanded short multiplication method

```
  10 + 3
 ×     7
 ───────
    7 0      10 × 7
    2 1       3 × 7
 ───────
    9 1
```

```
    1 3
 ×    7
 ──────
   7 0
   2 1
 ──────
   9 1
```

The short multiplication method

```
   13
 ×  7
 ────
```

    1 3   *Multiply from the right: i.e. multiply the units digits together.*

         $3 \times 7 = 21$

         Write down the 1 in the units column and the 2 (for 2 tens) in the tens column

   × 7   *Next multiply the tens digit in 13 by the 7*

         $10 \times 7 = 70$.

         Thus there are 7 tens plus the 2 tens already entered in the tens column making a total of 9 tens.

```
 9₂ 1
```

$13 \times 7 = 91$

2 Work out 347×28.

There are two ways of doing this:

The vertical layout method

```
      3  4  7
  ×      2  8
  ─────────────
  2  7₃ 7₅ 6     This line shows 347 × 8
  6  9₁ 4  0     This line shows 347 × 20
  ─────────────
  9  7  1  6
```

$347 \times 28 = 9716$

The grid method

×	300	40	7
20	6000	800	140
8	2400	320	56

Adding along each row gives:

6940

2776

Total 9716

3 Work out $52 \div 4$.
$$\begin{array}{r} 13 \\ 4\overline{)5^12} \end{array}$$

4 Work out $162 \div 6$.
$$\begin{array}{r} 27 \\ 6\overline{)16^42} \end{array}$$

5 Multiply 12 by $3\frac{3}{4}$.

First change $3\frac{3}{4}$ into an improper fraction: $\frac{15}{4}$.

Then multiply this by 12 and simplify:

$$12 \times \frac{15}{4} = \frac{156}{4} = 39$$

6 Find $\frac{1}{8}$ of £32.

$$£32 \times \frac{1}{8} = £4$$

Key facts

Set out calculations as larger number × smaller number.

The grid method is a useful method of multiplying – and one that you may use in secondary school. Both methods, (the grid method and the vertical layout method), rely on the fact that a number can be broken into parts. For example, 9×27 can be written as $9 \times (20 + 7)$ which equals $9 \times 20 + 9 \times 7 = 180 + 63 = 243$.

Language

Total the answer to an addition

Remainder the amount that is left over when doing a division

$$\begin{array}{r} 270 \\ 150 + \\ \hline 420 \end{array}$$

$$\begin{array}{r} 420 \\ 4 \times \\ \hline 1680 \end{array}$$

On track

1 There are 270 seats in Theatre 1 and 150 more seats in Theatre 2.

   a) How many seats are there in Theatre 2? 420

   Both theatres are open from Wednesday to Saturday. One week both theatres are full each day they are open.

   b) How many people went to shows at the theatres that week? 1680

2 Write the missing digits to make this correct.

$$\begin{array}{r} \boxed{2}\ 5\ \boxed{6} \\ \times \qquad\quad 7 \\ \hline 1\ 7\ 9\ 2 \end{array}$$

3 Work out:

   a) 52 × 4 208   **b)** 52 × 10 520   **c)** 52 × 24 1248
   d) 530 ÷ 10 530   **e)** 848 ÷ 8 6   **f)** 395 ÷ 5

4 Work out:

   a) 188 ÷ 7   **b)** 264 ÷ 8   **c)** 1234 ÷ 4   **d)** 4331 ÷ 3

5 Multiply:

   a) 24 by $1\frac{1}{2}$ **b)** 45 by $2\frac{3}{5}$

Aiming higher

1 261 children and 27 teachers go on a coach trip. How many 49-seater coaches does the school need to hire?

2 Maria and her sister want to buy a present for their mother.
   Maria has £17. Her sister has double that amount.
   They want to buy their mother a coat that costs £60. How much more money do they need?

3 Carpet tiles are sold in boxes of 10 tiles.
   Amy needs 123 carpet tiles.
   How many boxes should she buy?
   How many files will she have left over?

4 Trainers cost £60 per pair. How much do eight pairs cost?

5 18 people are going on a journey by taxi. Each taxi can take five people.
   How many taxis are needed?

6 Three friends buy a bag of sweets. There are 47 sweets in the bag.
They share them out equally. How many will each have?

7 A minibus can carry nine people. 88 people are going on a trip.
How many minibuses are needed?

8 Find:

a) $\dfrac{3}{4}$ of £10   b) $\dfrac{3}{20}$ of £100

9 Complete these calculations by writing in the missing numbers in the boxes.

a) $8 \times 34 = 8 \times (30 + 4) = \boxed{} + 32 = 272$

b) $6 \times 54 = 6 \times (\boxed{} + 4) = \boxed{} + 24 = \boxed{}$

c) $7 \times 86 = 7 \times (\boxed{} + \boxed{}) = 560 + \boxed{} = 602$

Using and applying

1 What is the total mass of 565 screws each weighing 9 g?

2 Find a number between 450 and 460 that gives a remainder of 5 when divided
by 8. How did you find the number?

3 Here is a number pattern.

1	$7 \times 9 + 37$	$= 100$
2	$7 \times 19 + 67$	$= 200$
3	$7 \times 29 + 97$	$= 300$
4	$7 \times 39 + 127$	$= 400$
5		

a) What calculation should be written in
line 5? Check the answer.

b) What calculation in this pattern will
have 700 as the answer?

4 How many tins, each 6 cm wide will fit on a shelf 100 cm long?

5 Here is a division grid.
Make sure you understand how it works.

÷	2	3	5
30	15	10	6
90	45	30	18
60	30	20	12

Copy and complete these division grids.

a)

÷	2	8	4
64	32	8	16
		10	
32		8	

b)

÷			8
8	4	2	1
		8	
80	20		

c)

÷	5	
30		10
120	24	12
		50

12 Factors and multiples

What will you learn?

How to:

● identify multiples and factors including finding all factor pairs.

I need to be able to:

● multiply and divide by numbers up to 20

● recognise simple factors and multiples.

Examples

Here are six number cards.

1 Which two numbers on the cards are factors of 42?
Now write down two common multiples of 4 and 12. These numbers are not on the cards.

> *3 and 7*
>
> *12 and 24*
>
> *Common multiples are numbers that are in the 4 and 12 times tables,*
>
> *so 24, 36, 48 are common multiples.*

2 What are the factors of 64?

> *You can find all the factors by considering 'factor pairs'.*
>
> *The first is* $1 \times 64 = 64$
>
> *Then* $2 \times 32 = 64$
>
> *3 won't be part of a factor pair because 3 doesn't divide into 64*
>
> $4 \times 16 = 64$
>
> $8 \times 8 = 64$
>
> *So the factors of 64 are 1, 64, 2, 32, 4, 16, 8*
>
> *Put them into order:*
>
> *1, 2, 4, 8, 16, 32, 64*

Key facts

The factors of a number are any whole numbers (integers) that divide into the number exactly.
A multiple of a number is a number you get from the first number by multiplication.
For example because 66 = 6 × 11. We can say that 66 is a multiple of 6 and 66 is a multiple of 11.

Language

Factors of a number are any whole numbers (integers) that divide into the number exactly. This includes 1 and the number itself. For example, the factors of 12 are 1, 2, 3, 4, 6, 12
Common factors are common to more than 1 number so that, for example, 2 is a common factor of 6 and 12
Common multiple a number that is a multiple of 2 or more numbers is a common multiple. For example, 15 and 30 are common multiples of 5

On track

1 Which of the following numbers are factors of 48?

2, 3, 4, 6, 8, 10, 12, 14, 16, 18, 20

2 Show how you would use factors to:

a) multiply 18 by 15.　　　b) divide 108 by 12.

3 Write down all the factors of 24.

6, 4, 1, 24, 2, 12, 3, 8,

4 List any four multiples of 7 which are less than 100.

77, 14, 49, 42,

5 Which of these is not a multiple of 3?

9　(26)　60　15　39　(38)　48　27

6 Which of these numbers has 9 as a factor?

33　(36)　48　17　(63)　(27)　(72)

7 Which numbers are factors of both 12 and 18? 6, 2, 3

8 Write down three common multiples of 4 and 6. 24, 36 48

Aiming higher

1 Lucy and John are playing a game with a set of cards. Each card has a number between 1 and 36 on it. Lucy takes a card and John has to work out what number is on the card. He uses the following facts that Lucy has given him:

- 3 is a factor of the number
- the sum of the digits in the number lies between 4 and 8
- it is an odd number
- When the digits are multiplied together the total lies between 4 and 8.

*41 33 34 43
32 34 2 52 29
50 5   61 16
23 68 70*

What is the number on Lucy's card? *15*

2 Two numbers are in the wrong place in this diagram. Which two numbers are they? Copy the diagram with the numbers in the correct place.

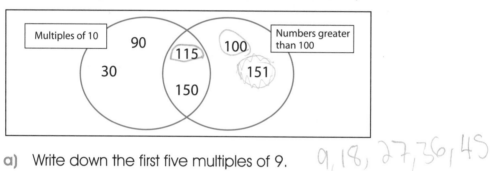

Multiples of 10   90   115   100   Numbers greater than 100
30   151
150

3 a) Write down the first five multiples of 9. *9, 18, 27, 36, 45*

b) Can you see a pattern in these multiples? *yes*

4 Complete these sentences correctly by using the words 'factors' or 'multiples'.

a) 12 is one of the ...*multiples*... of 6.

b) 4 is one of the ...*factors*... of 12.

c) 6 and 3 are both ...*factors*... of 18.

d) 30 and 10 are both ...*multiples*... of 5.

5 Write down the common factors of 12, 24 and 36. *6, 4, 3, 12*

6 Look at the numbers 12, 24, 30, 36, 60.

Which of these numbers are multiples of both?

a) 2 and 3 *12, 30, 36, 24, 60*

b) 3 and 4 *12, 24, 36, 60*

c) 4 and 5 *5 60*

d) 5 and 6 *60, 30*

e) 7 and 8

7 Find the common factors of:

a) 45 and 60   b) 36 and 54

15, 3, 5, 1   *9, 1, 2, 18, 6, 3*

Using and applying

1 Write down three common multiples for 4, 6 and 8. How did you find them?

24, 48, 72   doubled 24

2 Spiders have 8 legs and insects have 6 legs. In a group of spiders and flies, there are 46 legs.

   a) How many spiders and flies are there? *5 spiders 1 fly*

      Hint: This a question about multiples.

   b) What if there were 72 legs? *6 spiders 4 flies*

3 Milly and Ewan are brother and sister. Milly visits Grandma every four days; Ewan visits Grandma every five days. If they visit both visit Grandma today, how many days will it be before they both visit Grandma on the same day?

20 days

4 Find the factors of:

   a) 13 *1, 13*   b) 19 *1, 19*   c) 31 *1, 31*   d) 37 *1, 37*

   e) What do you notice about the answers to a–d? *they're all with one only*

   f) What is the special name given to numbers like this? *prime numbers*

5 A perfect number is a number that is equal to the sum of its factors not counting the number itself. The first perfect number is 6, because 1, 2, and 3 are the factors, not counting 6, and 1 + 2 + 3 = 6. The next perfect number is 28 because 1 + 2 + 4 + 7 + 14 = 28. After 28 the next two numbers are 496 and 8128.

'sort of perfect numbers' are more common. These are numbers that can be divided by their digits and by the sum of their digits.

- 12 is a 'sort of perfect number' because 12 is divisible by 1, 2 and 3 and 3 = 1 + 2

- 24 is a 'sort of perfect number' because it is divisible by 2, 4 and 6 and 6 = 2 + 4

Try to find some more 'sort of perfect numbers' which are less than 100.

Hint: Think about multiples of 12

36 48 60 72 84 96

13 Squares and cubes

What will you learn?

How to:

- recognise and use square numbers and cube numbers and the notation for square and cube.

I need to know:

- the multiplication tables up to 10×10.

Example

1 What is 6^2?

  6^2 is 6×6 so the answer is 36.

Key facts

You can make a square number by multiplying any number by itself.
E.g. $15^2 = 15 \times 15 = 225$ and 225 is a square number.

A **cube number** is found by multiplying the number by itself and then by itself again.

You show that a number is squared by adding a small raised 2 after the number, so for 3 squared you would write 3^2 and say it as '3 squared'.

Similarly, you show that a number is cubed by adding a small raised 3 after the number for 4 cubed. You would write 4^3 and say it as '4 cubed'. (The answer is $4 \times 4 \times 4 = 64$)

Language

Squaring number a number that can be drawn as a square array of dots
squaring multiplying a number by itself

A **square number** is the product of two identical whole numbers. Square numbers can be represented by dots arranged in a square, so 3^2 would be

On track

1. Work out: 49
   a) 7^2 44
   b) 11^2 121 131 22
   c) 4^3 64
   d) 5^3 125 45

2. The missing numbers are all square numbers. Find the square numbers
   a) $\boxed{16} + \boxed{9} = 25$
   b) $\boxed{144} + \boxed{25} = 169$
   c) $\boxed{16} \times \boxed{9} = 144$

Aiming higher

1. Look at this pattern.

   $1 + 3 = 2^2$

   $1 + 3 + 5 = 3^2$

   $1 + 3 + 5 + 7 = 4^2$

   a) What do you notice?

   b) Use the pattern to copy and complete this number sentence.

   $1 + 3 + 5 + 7 + 9 + 11 + 13 = \boxed{7}^2 = \boxed{49}$

2. Odd square numbers can be made by adding two consecutive numbers.

   E.g. $3^2 = 4 + 5$ $5^2 = 12 + 13$ $7^2 = 24 + 25$

   a) What number squared = 60 + 61? 11^2

   b) What two consecutive numbers add to give 13^2? $84 + 85$

Using and applying

1. Arash rolls two dice.

   One dice is numbered 1 to 6 and the other is numbered 3 to 8.

   The two rolled numbers are used to make a two-digit number.

   E.g. 35 or 53

   Which square numbers could Arash make?   16, 25, 36

2. Here are ten number cards:

   | 1 | 2 | 3 | 4 | 5 | 6 | 7 | 8 | 9 | 10 |

   Place the cards in pairs so that, when you add them, each total is a square number.

   E.g. $\boxed{4} + \boxed{5}$ which is a square number ($9 = 3^2$)

   How many other pairs can you find? $8+1, 6+3, 9+7, 8+8, 1+3, 7+2$

14 Prime numbers

What will you learn?

How to:

- know and use the vocabulary of prime numbers, prime factors and composite numbers

- establish whether a number up to 100 is prime and recall the prime numbers up to 19.

Be able to:

- find pairs of factors of 2-digit numbers.

Example

1 Find the prime factors of 36.

You can use a factor tree to find the prime factors of a number.

Here is the factor tree for 36.

Begin with 36 at the top.

Underneath write a factor pair for 36,

e.g. 12 and 3.

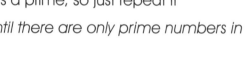

If either factor is not prime, continue by writing another factor pair underneath

e.g. 3 and 4 below 12.   **Hint:** 3 is a prime, so just repeat it

Keep drawing the tree like this until there are only prime numbers in the bottom row.

So 36 = 3 × 2 × 2 × 3, and the prime factors of 36 are 2 and 3.

Key fact

A prime number has exactly two factors, which means it can only be divided exactly by itself and 1. The number 1 is not a prime number because it has only one factor.

Language

Factors are numbers that divide **exactly** into other numbers (no remainder), e.g. 3 is a factor of 6 because 3 divides exactly into 6

Prime factors are the factors that are prime numbers

On track

6,2   7,7   10,2,5,4?

1   a)   Write down the factors of 12, 14 and 20, and then 4, 9 and 16.

    b)   What do you notice about the number of factors each of the square
         numbers has?

    c)   Investigate some more square numbers.

2   a)   Copy and complete this factor tree for 56.

    b)   Now write down the prime factors of 56.

3   List the prime factors of 60.

4   Is 21 a prime number?
    Give a reason for your answer.

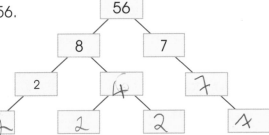

Aiming higher

1   a)   The number 1 is not a prime number. Can you explain why?

    b)   Are there any even prime numbers apart from 2? Can you explain why?

2   13 is a prime number and so is 31.
    List all the other two-digit prime numbers that are still prime when their digits are
    reversed.

3   List all the prime numbers that are less than 20.

4   a)   Write down 2 consecutive numbers that are prime.

    b)   Write down 2 consecutive odd numbers, less than 20, that are prime.

Using and applying

1   Find three prime numbers to multiply together to give a product of:

    a)   105   b)   385.

    Show how you worked out your answers.

2

20 = 3 + 17

16 = 3 + 13

I think I can
make any number
that isn't a prime number
by adding two prime
numbers.

Try some other numbers and see if you think this is always possible.

15 Estimating and drawing angles

What will you learn?

- That angles are measured in degrees.
- How to estimate and measure angles and draw a given angle, writing its size in degrees.
- How to identify:
  - multiples of 90°
  - and angles at a point on a straight line and ½ turn total 180°
  - and angles at a point and one whole turn total 360°
  - reflex angles
  - and compare different angles.

I need to know how to:

- draw lines accurately
- read the scale on a ruler and on a protractor or angle measurer
- recognise acute, obtuse and right angles.

Examples

1 Which of these angles are acute and which are obtuse? Estimate the size of each angle and then measure each angle.

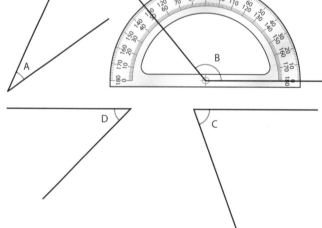

A, C and D are acute; B is obtuse.

A is 30°, B is 130°, C is 70° and D is 45°.

2 Find the size of the missing angle in this drawing.

78°

Angles on a straight line add up to 180°.
180° − 78° = 102°, so the missing angle is 102°.

3 Find the size of the
   third angle in this
   drawing.

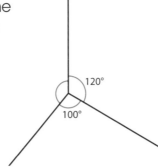

The angles round a point add up to 360°.

100° + 120° = 220°, so the third angle is

360° – 220° = 140°.

Key fact

Acute angles are less than 90°; obtuse angles are greater than 90° and less than 180°.
Angles on a straight line add up to 180°.
Angles round a point add up to 360°.

Language

Acute angles   are less than 90°
Obtuse angles   are greater than 90° and less than 180°
Reflex angles   are angles greater than 180°

On track

1 This is a six-sided star.

   Measure angles **a** and **b** accurately.

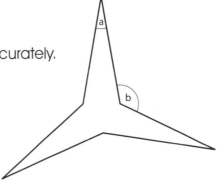

2 **RS** is a straight line.

   Calculate the size of angle **a**.

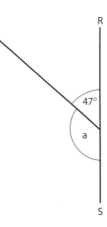

3 Work out the missing angle in each of these drawings.

a)

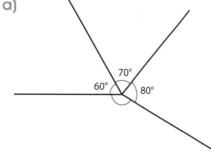

70°
60° 80°

b)

these 2 angles
are equal

120° 80°

Aiming higher

1 Copy and complete the table below about the angles
in the star.

Put a tick in the correct box depending on whether the
angle is acute or obtuse.

Estimate, in degrees, the size of each angle and then
measure the angles.

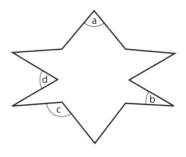

Angle	Acute angle	Obtuse angle	Estimate of size in degrees	Actual size in degrees
a	✓			
b	✓✓		✓	
c		✓		
d	✓			

2 Identify which of these angles are acute, obtuse or reflex?

a) 57° b) 110° c) 195°

d) 28° e) 124° f) 345°

g) 91° h) 222° j) 6°

Using and applying

1 **AB** is a straight line.

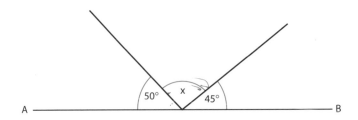

Calculate the size of angle **x**.

2 a) Measure the angles in this shape.

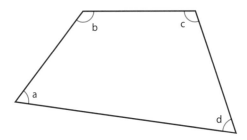

b) Which of the angles are obtuse?

c) Add together the sizes of angle a and angle b.

d) Add together the sizes of angle c and angle d.

e) Add together these two answers. How close to 360° is your answer?

3 Look at the clock face.

Does the hour hand turn through an acute angle, a right angle, an obtuse angle or a reflex angle when it moves

a) from 12 noon to 3 p.m.

b) from 2 p.m. to 7 p.m.

c) from 10 a.m. to 1 p.m.

d) from 8 a.m. to 5 p.m.?

16 Properties of shape

What will you learn?

How to:

● state and use the properties of a rectangle (including squares) to deduce related facts

● distinguish between regular and irregular polygons based on reasoning about equal sides and angles

● identify and name the following: parallelogram, rhombus, trapezium.

I need to be able to:

● recognise parallel lines and perpendicular lines in shapes.

Examples

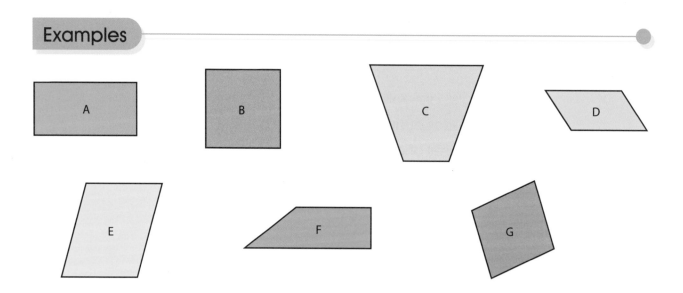

1 Which of these quadrilaterals is a:

square?	rectangle?	parallelogram?	trapezium?	rhombus?
B	A	D, E	C, F	G

2 Which of the quadrilaterals have two pairs of parallel lines?

square, rectangle, parallelogram, rhombus

Key facts

A **regular shape** has all its sides of equal length and all its angles of equal size.

An **irregular shape** does not have sides of equal length and the angles are not all the same size.

A **scalene triangle** has three sides of different length.

An **isosceles triangle** has two sides the same length.

An **equilateral triangle** has three sides all the same length.

A **right-angled triangle** has one of its angles equal to 90° – a right angle. A right-angled triangle can also be an isosceles triangle.

For the next facts look at the diagrams in the examples.

A **rectangle** has four sides. The opposite sides are equal and parallel. All the angles in a rectangle are 90°. A square is a special rectangle; the difference is that all the sides are equal in length.

A **parallelogram** is like a 'pushed-over' rectangle. The opposite sides are equal and parallel but the angles are not 90°.

A **rhombus** is like a pushed-over square, or like a parallelogram with sides of equal length.

A **trapezium** is a four-sided shape where only one pair of sides is parallel.

Language

Vertex   (plural vertices) a corner of a shape
Parallel lines   two lines that are the same distance apart along their whole length

On track

1   Triangle A has sides 10 cm, 12 cm, 6 cm.

Triangle B has sides 8 cm, 10 cm, 8 cm.

Triangle C has sides 20 cm, 30 cm, 20 cm.

Triangle D has sides 6 cm, 6 cm, 6 cm.

Which triangles are:

a) scalene   b) isosceles   c) equilateral?

A   C B   D

2   List the shapes that have:

   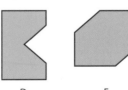

A   B   C   D   E   F

a)   two sets of two parallel lines A C   b)   two sets of three parallel lines

c)   three sets of two parallel lines. D

3 Copy and complete each sentence with the name of the correct triangle.

In an _____ triangle all three sides are equal in length and all three angles are equal in size.

An _____ triangle has only two equal sides and two equal angles.

In a _____ triangle no two sides or angles are equal.

In a _____ triangle one of the angles is a right angle.

4 Ashok draws a four-sided figure. The angles are all 90°. One pair of sides is 10 cm long and the other pair of sides is 5 cm long. Ashok says the shape he has drawn is regular. Is he right?

5 Which of these shapes has five equal sides?

A regular pentagon   **B** regular hexagon   **C** regular octagon

Aiming higher

1 Name and describe shapes A to E as fully as you can.

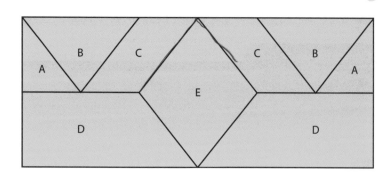

2 **a)** Write the correct name under each of these triangles. Choose from this list:

equilateral   isosceles   right-angled   scalene

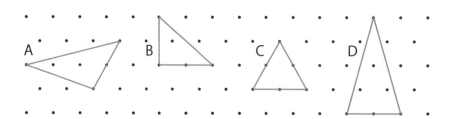

b) Which of these triangles is regular?

3 **a)** How many equilateral triangles would fit together to make this hexagon?

b) What sort of hexagon is it?

c) What size is each angle?

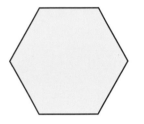

4 Keisha says that all these shapes are regular.

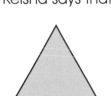  

Is she correct? Write down the reasons for your answers.

Using and applying

1 Is it possible for a quadrilateral to have exactly three right angles? Why not?

2 The quadrilateral has vertices A, B, C and D.

A is the point (2, 4), B is (6, 4), C is (10, 6) and D is (5, 7).

By moving one point, can you change the shape into:

a) a parallelogram? **b)** a triangle?

Write down the name of the point you are moving and the position it moves to.

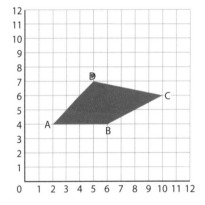

3 **a)** Which of the angles in the box below are acute angles?

b) Which angles could never be in a triangle?

15°	115°	67°	108°
68°	323°	206°	200°
98°	289°	131°	180°

4 The three angles of a triangle are each 60°.

Is the triangle regular? What kind of triangle is it?

17 Drawing shapes

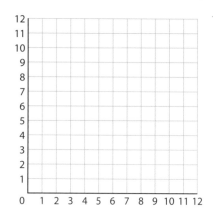

What will you learn?

How to:

● measure, draw and compare angles knowing that they are measured in degrees

● identify 3-D shapes including cubes and cuboids from 2-D representations.

I need to know:

● how to use a protractor and how to measure accurately using a ruler.

Examples

1 Draw a square with sides 6 cm long.

If you are using squared paper this is easy:

Choose a point where the grid lines cross. Measure 6 cm along a line from this point and 6 cm up a line. Then repeat this at the other end of the line.

> *If you are using plain paper then:*

● *Draw a line across the paper 6 cm long.*
  Remember to start at 0 on the ruler, not from the end of the ruler.

● *At one end, using your protractor mark where the 90 point is. (Make sure you have your protractor placed accurately on the paper.) Then join the end of the line to the point marked and extend the line until it is 6 cm long.*

● *Continue around the paper making the square.*

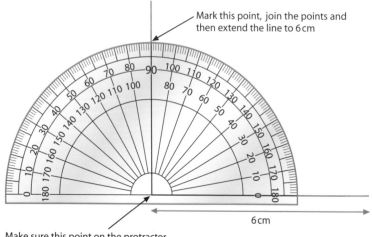

Mark this point, join the points and then extend the line to 6 cm

6 cm

Make sure this point on the protractor is exactly at the end of the line

2 Are these two shapes the same?

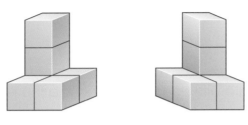

This shape is made from 6 cubes, though you can only see 5 of them.

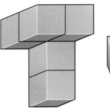
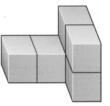

This shape can also be rotated but it stays as the same shape.

*The shape could also be reflected: it is similar but it is **not** the same.*

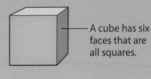

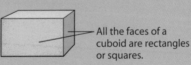

This shape can be rotated (spun around) but it stays as the same shape.

Key facts

A rectangle has four sides. The opposite sides are equal and parallel. All the angles in a rectangle are 90°. The diagonals cut each other in half.

A square is a special rectangle – the difference is that all the sides are equal in length. The diagonals cut each other in half and the angles between the diagonals are 90°.

This is a **cuboid**. — All the faces of a cuboid are rectangles or squares.

This is a **cube**. — A cube has six faces that are all squares.

Language

Vertex (plural vertices)   a corner of a 2-D or a 3-D shape

Parallel lines   two lines that are the same distance apart along their whole length. Lines that are parallel are often shown with small arrows to indicate that they are parallel.

Face   the flat side of a 3-D object

On track

1   Draw a square with sides 8 cm. Measure the length of a diagonal.

2   Draw a rectangle with sides of 6 cm and 8 cm. Measure the length of a diagonal.

3   How many faces, edges and vertices does a cuboid have?   6   12   6   17

4   This picture shows a set of steps.

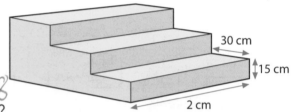

a)   What solid shapes could they be
made from?   Cuboid

b)   How many vertical edges are there?   8

c)   How many horizontal edges are there?

5   Draw a right-angled triangle with sides 6 cm, 8 cm and 10 cm.
The right angle is between the 6 cm and 8 cm sides.
Measure the other angles.

6   This is a sketch of a triangle but it is not the
right size.

Draw this triangle as accurately as you can.
Measure the length of the third side.

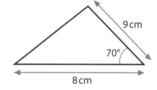

9 cm

70°

8 cm

 Aiming higher

1   Copy and complete the table. One box has been filled in for you already.

	Sides		Diagonals	Parallel sides		Angles	
Quadrilateral	4 equal sides	2 different pairs of equal sides	Equal diagonals	2 pairs of parallel sides	Only one pair of parallel sides	All angles equal	Only pairs of opposite angles equal
Square	✓		✓	✓		✓	
Rectangle							

2   How many faces, edges and vertices does a cube have?

3   Draw a regular pentagon with sides 6 cm long. Remember that the angle between
the sides is 120°.

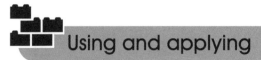

Using and applying

1 These two solids are made from cubes.

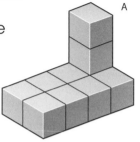

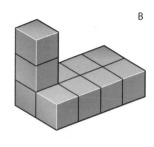

Make sure you can see what the difference is between solid A and solid B.
Match A or B with each of these drawings.

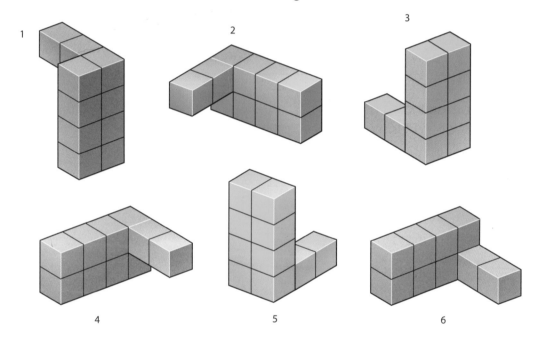

number	shape
1	B
2	A
3	B
4	A
5	B
6	A

18 Reflecting shapes

What will you learn?

How to:

- identify, describe and represent the position of a shape following a reflection using the appropriate vocabulary and know that the shape will not change.

I need to be able to:

- use co-ordinates in the first quadrant
- recognise shapes with line symmetry.

Example

1 Write down the co-ordinates of the triangle after reflection in the mirror line.

(7, 2) (9, 1) (9, 3)

Remember that the co-ordinates of a point are given in the order (x co-ordinate, y co-ordinate). So the top left-hand corner of the blue triangle is at the point (1, 3).

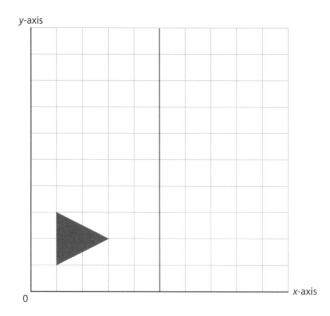

Key facts

In a reflection, every point on the original shape (the object) is reflected to a point at an equal distance on the other side of the mirror line.

If a mirror is placed along a line on a diagram and the shape still looks the same, then the mirror line is a line of reflective symmetry.

Language

Reflection   a 'flip over' movement in a mirror line

Symmetry   a shape has (line) symmetry if a mirror line can be placed so that the shape on one side reflects exactly onto the other side

Transformation   the movement of a shape by translation, reflection or rotation

On track

1 The heavy lines are lines of symmetry. Copy and complete the pattern.

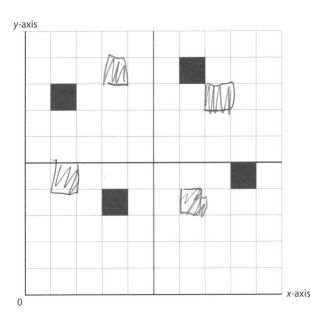

2 The white triangle is a reflection of the shaded triangle. Write down the co-ordinates of the white triangle.

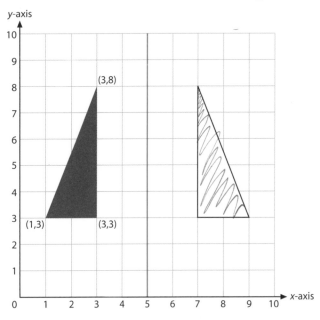

3 Harry has drawn the reflection of flag A in the mirror line.

He labels its reflection B. His teacher marks it wrong.

Copy these possible reasons for it being wrong.

• Flag B is facing the wrong way.

• The arrow on flag B is facing the wrong way.

• Flag B is too close to the mirror line.

Think about each one and write *true* or *false* next to it.

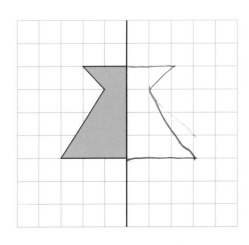

4 Copy the shape and the mirror line onto squared paper.

Draw the reflection of the shape in the mirror line.

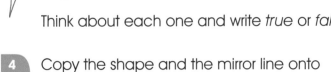

Aiming higher

1 Here is a shaded square on a grid. Copy and shade in three more squares so that the design is symmetrical in both mirror lines.

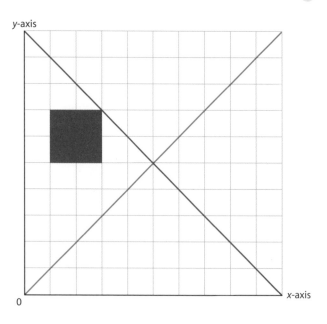

2 Copy this diagram onto squared paper and reflect the shape in the mirror line.

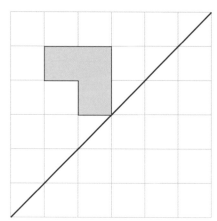

3 Which of these shapes has been reflected in the mirror line?.

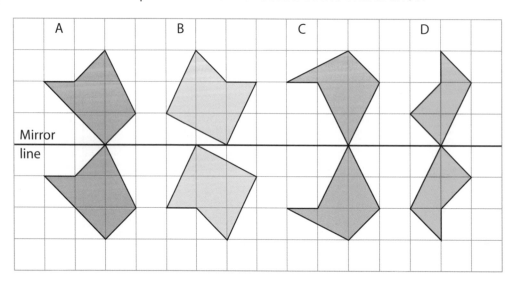

Using and applying

1 All of the L-shapes are identical.

Write down a transformation that moves the first shape onto the second shape:

a) A to B **b)** A to D **c)** A to C

There are three different transformations that will move A onto C. Can you find them all?

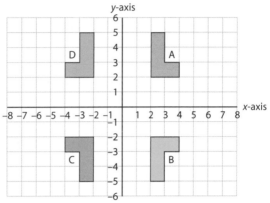

2 Complete the diagram below to make a shape that is symmetrical about both mirror lines.

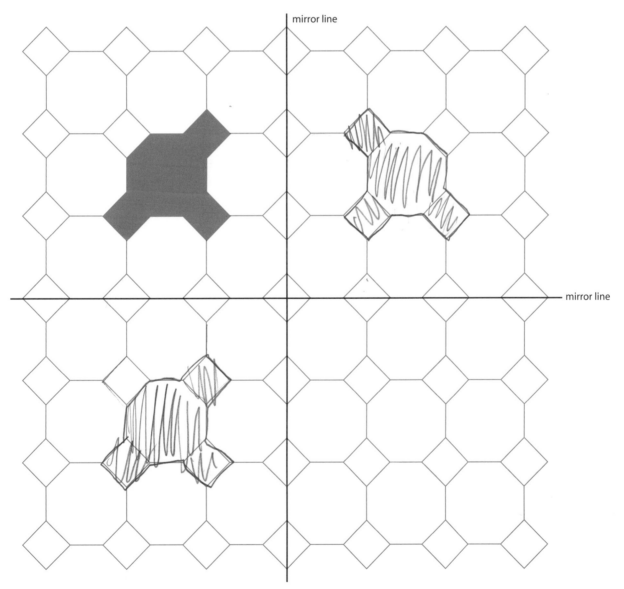

19 Translating shapes

What will you learn?

How to:

- identify, describe and represent the position of a shape following a translation, using the appropriate vocabulary, and know that the shape will not change
- how to recognise if a shape has been translated or reflected.

I need to be able to:

- use co-ordinates in the first quadrant.

Example

Triangles A, B and C show the position of triangle X after a translation or a reflection.

Describe the transformations.

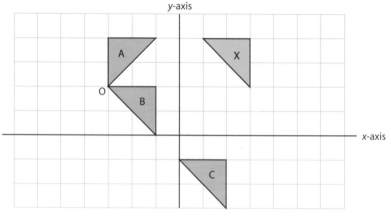

*Triangle C is a **translation** of triangle X, 1 square to the left and 5 squares down.*

*Triangle A is a **reflection** of triangle X in the y-axis. Notice that triangle A and triangle X are symmetrical about the y-axis.*

The y-axis is the line of reflective symmetry.

*Triangle B is a **translation** of triangle X, 4 squares to the left and 2 squares down.*

Key fact

A translation is described or given by the distance moved to the left or right and the distance moved up or down.

Language

Translation   a move or a slide to the left or right and/or up and down, with no turning or reflection

On track

1 Draw the position of this triangle after it has been translated 4 squares to the right and 3 squares down.

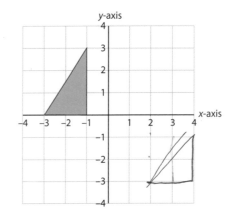

Aiming higher

1 The shaded shape is translated by 4 squares across and 1 square down.

a) Which of the shapes A, B or C shows the correct translation?

b) How would you write down the translation for the other two shapes?

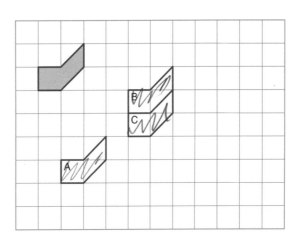

Using and applying

1 a) Explain how to translate shape A so that it covers shape B.

b) How would you translate shape B so that it covers shape A? What do you notice?

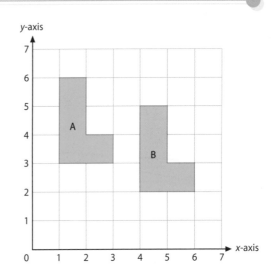

20 Time and length, weight and capacity with metric units

What will you learn?

How to:

- solve problems involving addition, subtraction, multiplication and division of units of measure (e.g. length, mass, volume, money) using decimal notation
- understand and use the basic equivalences between metric and common imperial units and express them in approximate terms
- solve problems involving converting between units of time
- solve problems involving converting between units of measure (e.g. kilometre and metre, metre and centimetre, centimetre and millimetre, kilogram and gram, litre and millilitre)

I need to be able to:

- multiply and divide by 10, 100, 1000
- read scales on measuring instruments accurately
- measure accurately
- change from mm to cm or from cm to m, etc.
- count up or multiply by 24 and by 60.

Examples

1 This simple map shows three towns and the shortest straight line distances, in kilometres, between their centres.

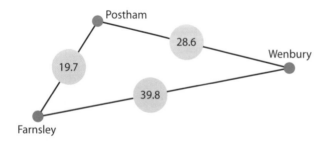

What is the total distance from Postham to Wenbury then to Farnsley?

28.6 + 39.8 = 68.4 km

2 Change these lengths in metres into millimetres.

a) 2.435 metres   **b)** 3.52 metres

Remember that there are 1000 mm in a metre so you will multiply each measurement by 1000.

a) 2.435 m × 1000 = 2435 mm   b) 3.52 m × 1000 = 3520 mm

3 How many minutes are there between a quarter to ten and twenty five past ten?

From a quarter to ten to 10 o'clock is 15 minutes. From 10 o'clock to 25 past 10 is 25 minutes. Total time is 15 + 25 = 40 minutes.

Key facts

10 mm in 1 cm	100 cm in 1 m	1000 m in 1 km
1000 g in 1 kg	1000 ml in 1 l	

Some approximate conversions between metric and Imperial units are:

From	To	
Centimetres	Inches	Multiply by 5 then divide by 2
Litres	Pints	Multiply by 7 then divide by 4
Kilometres	Miles	Multiply by 5 and divide by 8
Metres	Feet	Multiply by 10 and divide by 3
Inches	Centimetres	Multiply by 2 then divide by 5
Pints	Litres	Multiply by 4 then divide by 7
Miles	Kilometres	Multiply by 8 then divide by 5
Feet	Metres	Multiply by 3 and divide by 10
Kilograms	Pounds	Multiply by 2.2

There are 60 seconds	in a minute.
There are 60 minutes	in an hour.
There are 24 hours	in a day.
There are 30 or 31 days	in a month except for February, which has 28 days or 29 days in a leap year.
There are 12 months	in a year.

Language

centi... in measurement 'centi' means a hundredth, e.g. one centimetre is a hundredth of a metre

kilo... in measurement 'kilo' means a thousand, e.g. one kilometre is a thousand metres

On track

26.5g

1 a) Write 26.5 kg in grams.   b) Write 7 kg 300 g as a decimal.

2 How many glasses each holding 150 ml can be filled from this jug of orange juice?

3 Add these lengths: 2.5 cm, 7.65 cm and 13.9 cm.

4 Add these weights: 360 g, 20 g and 1.25 kg.

5 Change these metric measurements into their approximate Imperial equivalents:

a)   10 litres   b)   200 kilograms   c)   100 km

6 a) Write 8 kilograms 50 grams as a decimal.

b) How many centimetres make 3.6 m?

7 How many days are there between 1st October and 31st December?

8 How many seconds are there in 3 minutes and 40 seconds?

9 How many minutes are there between

a) quarter to 7 and 20 past 7?   b) 25 to 9 and half past 9?

10 A paperback book weighs 250g. How much will 13 copies of the book weigh? Give your answer both in grams and kilograms.

11 5 bars of chocolate weigh 2kg. How much does 1 bar weigh?

Aiming higher

1 A tin of rice pudding weighs 425 g. How many grams less than 1 kg is this?

2 Put these lengths in order, the shortest first:

$\frac{1}{2}$ m   1.2 km   3 cm   25 mm

3 Here are some facts from a book of records printed some years ago.

For each fact, change the Imperial units into metric units.

a) The largest champagne bottle holds 26 pints.

b) Racing pigeons can reach speeds of 60 miles per hour.

c) A Great Dane can be over 36 inches tall at the shoulder and weigh more than 180 pounds.

d) The world's tallest person was 108 inches tall.

e) The longest seat in the world is 39 feet long.

4 The time on Simon's digital watch is 18:02. Simon's watch is seven minutes fast. How should the correct time be displayed?

5 A plank of wood 1.75 m long is cut into 5 equal lengths. How long is each piece?

Using and applying

1 **a)** Which measure is equivalent to 1.3 l?

130 ml   1003 ml   1300 ml   103 ml

How do you know?

b) Which of these measurements is equivalent to 2.07 m?

270 cm   2007 cm   207 cm   270 cm

2 This earring is made from gold wire. Measure accurately the total length of gold wire in the earring. Give the units of your answer.

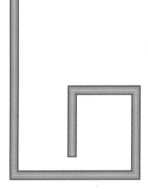

3 You have these weights:

5 g, 10 g, 20 g, 20 g, 50 g, 100 g, 200 g, 200 g, 500 g, 1 kg, 2 kg

Which of these weights could you use to weigh out or balance on scales these amounts?

a) 125 g   **b)** 560 g   **c)** 1.285 kg   **d)** 2090 g

4 **a)** What is the finishing time for a TV programme that starts at 1:35 p.m. and lasts for 40 minutes?

b) What is the start time for a TV programme that ends at 19:25 and lasts for 45 minutes?

5 A plane takes off on Wednesday at 22:57. It lands on Thursday at 06:05. How long is the flight in hours and minutes? Show how you calculated your answer.

21 Area and perimeter

What will you learn?

How to:

● calculate, estimate and compare the area of squares, rectangles and related composite shapes using standard units including cm² and m²

● calculate the perimeter of squares and rectangles

● estimate the area of irregular shapes.

I know how to:

● distinguish between area and perimeter.

Example

Find the area and perimeter of a rectangle with length 8.2 cm and width 5.2 cm.

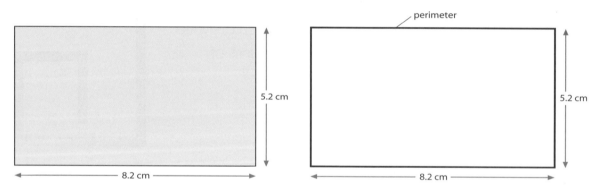

Area is length × width = 8.2 × 5.2 = 42.64 cm²

Perimeter is 2 × length + width   = 2 × (8.2 + 5.2)

= 2 × 13.4

= 26.8 cm

Key facts

The perimeter of a rectangle is its length + width + length + width. The units are centimetres (cm) or metres (m), etc.

The area of a rectangle is its length × width. The units are cm² or m², etc.

Language

Perimeter   of a rectangle is its length + width + length + width, or 2 × length + 2 × width

The units are centimetres, metres or kilometres, etc. (units of length)

Area   the amount of space covered by a shape

On track

1 What is the perimeter and area of a rectangle with length 11 m and width 4 m?

2 This is a picture of a flag. 30M

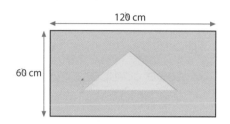

120 cm

60 cm

a) Work out its perimeter in metres.

b) Work out its area in cm².

c) 20% of the area of the flag is a triangle coloured yellow.

What is the area of the coloured triangle?

Aiming higher

1 What is the area of a rectangle measuring 43 cm by 34 cm? 1462 cm²

2 The area of a rectangle is 132 m². The shortest side is 6 m long. What is the length of the longest side?

3 Find the area and perimeter of this L shape.
Show how you calculated your answers.

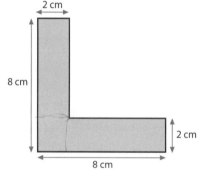

2 cm

8 cm

8 cm

2 cm

4 Estimate the area of the shape drawn on the centimetre square grid.

Hint: Count all the whole squares and any squares that are larger than a half square.

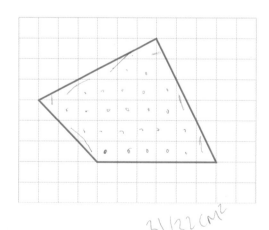

31/32 cm²

Using and applying

1 A rectangle has a perimeter of 42 m. The shortest side is 8 m long. What is the length of the longest side? How did you work it out?

2 The area of a rectangle is 24 cm². What are the lengths of the sides? Are there other possible answers?

22 Graphs and tables

What will you learn?

How to:

- solve comparison, sum and difference problems using information presented in line graphs
- complete, read and interpret information in tables, including timetables.

I need to be able to:

- plot and read graphs
- complete tables of information.

Examples

1 Here is part of a train timetable.

Edinburgh	–	09:35	–	–	13:35	–
Glasgow	09:15	–	11:15	13:15	–	13:45
Stirling	09:57	–	11:57	13:57	–	14:29
Perth	10:34	10:51	12:34	14:34	14:50	15:15
Inverness	–	13:10	–	–	17:05	–

How long does the first train from Glasgow to Perth take to travel?

Ellen is at Edinburgh station at 1:30 p.m. She wants to travel to Inverness. She catches the next train. At what time will she arrive in Inverness?

- *1 hour 19 minutes.*   - *17:05.*

2 Amy asked some people about their favourite fruits.

This bar chart shows how they answered.

Suggest two questions that you could ask about this data and give the answers to your questions.

- *How many people chose pears? (13)*
- *Which fruit was chosen by the fewest people? (apple)*
- *How many people did Amy ask? (52)*

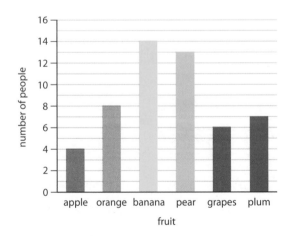

Key facts

a.m. is the time before 12 noon (midday); p.m. is the time from noon until midnight. In the 24-hour clock, time is given using four digits, for example, 07:05 for five past seven in the morning; or 17:10 for ten past five in the afternoon.

Graphs are useful to compare sets of data.

Language

See the **Key facts** for definitions of a.m. and p.m. and the 24-hour clock

Bar chart   see the question in **Example 2** opposite
Pie chart   see question 2 in **On track** for example
Graph   see question 1 in **On track** for example

On track

1   This graph shows the average monthly temperature in London.

   a)   What was the hottest month and what was the average temperature in that month?   July 25°c

   b)   Name two months in which the average temperature was the same.

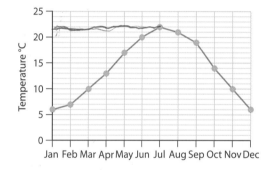

This graph shows the average monthly temperature in Amsterdam.

   c)   Write down two questions that allow you to compare the temperatures in both cities.

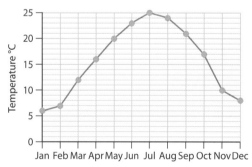

2   Here is the calendar for September 2013.

September					
M		2	9	16	23	30
T		3	10	17	24	
W		4	11	18	25	
T		5	12	19	26	
F		6	13	20	27	
S		7	14	21	28	
S	1	8	15	22	29	

   a)   Kathy's birthday is on 23rd September. She has a party on the Saturday after her birthday. What date is this?

   b)   Janet's birthday is on 27th September. What day of the week is this?

   c)   School starts on the first Monday in September. What date is this?

3 This line graph shows the temperature in a classroom through the day.

What was the temperature at 3 p.m. (15:00)?

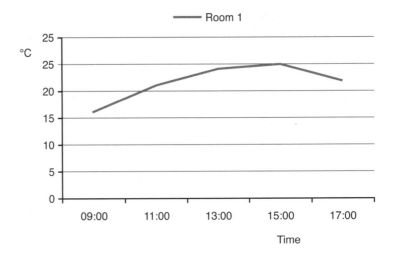

4 This graph shows the average temperature in London through the year.

In which two months was the temperature 20°C?

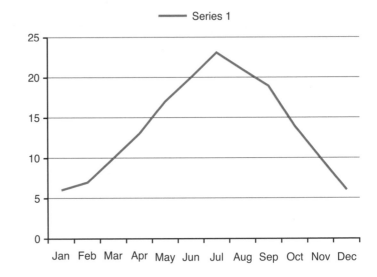

Aiming higher

1 Here is part of a timetable.

Newcastle	07:44	08:24	09:35	09:40	10:26
York	08:44	09:27	10:34	10:44	11:27
Leeds	09:10			11:10	
Wakefield	09:23			11:23	
Sheffield	09:53	10:23	11:23	11:53	12:23
Derby	10:24	10:57	11:57	12:24	12:57

a) Which train travels from Newcastle to York in the shortest time? And how long does it take?

b) Emma arrives at Newcastle station five minutes after the 07:44 train has left. She wants to go to Wakefield. How much longer does she have to wait for the next train?

2 This bar chart shows the total number of goals scored in each first-round match of the World Cup in South Africa in 2010.

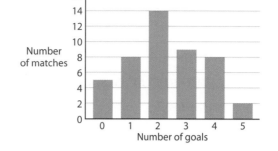

a) In how many matches were no goals scored?

b) In how many matches were less than three goals scored?

c) How many matches were played in the first round of the World Cup in South Africa in 2010?

3 Class 5 have done a shoe size survey.
Kylie has drawn a graph showing the results.

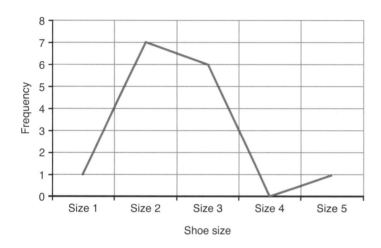

How many children had shoe size 2?

Using and applying

1 Amy has invented a dice game. It involves throwing two normal dice.

A person's score is the higher of the two numbers showing.

The score here is 5.

The score here is 3.

This bar line chart shows the scores Amy found after some throws.

a) Which score was the least frequent?

b) What was the total number of times Amy threw the two dice?

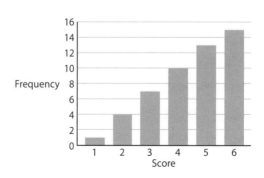

Glossary

Acute angles   are less than 90°

Area   the amount of space covered by a shape

Common factor   a factor which is a factor of two numbers

Common multiple   a number that is a multiple of at least two numbers

Cuboid   a solid with six faces that are rectangles. The opposite sides are exactly the same. Each edge is perpendicular to the edges that are joined to it.

Decimal place   is used with a number to show how many figures after the decimal point there are

Face   the flat side of a 3-D object

Factor   a number that divides exactly into another

Hundredths (h) $1\frac{1}{100}$ of a unit

Improper fraction   one where the numerator is greater than the denominator

Irregular shape   does not have sides of equal length and the angles are not all the same size.

Mixed number   a whole number and a fraction

Negative numbers   numbers less than zero

Obtuse angles   are greater than 90° and less than 180°

Parallel lines   two lines that are the same distance apart along their whole length

Perimeter   the distance around the edge of a shape

Positive numbers   numbers greater than zero

Prime factors   are the factors that are prime numbers

Proper fraction   one where the numerator is less than the denominator

Reflection   a 'flip over' movement in a mirror line

Reflex angles   are angles greater than 180°

Regular shape   has all its sides of equal length and all its angles of equal size

Remainder   the amount that is left over when doing a division

Simplify   to find an equivalent fraction with the smallest denominator possible

Square number   the product of two identical whole numbers

Symmetry   a shape has (line) symmetry if a mirror line can be placed so that the shape on one side reflects exactly onto the other side

Tenths (t) $1\frac{1}{10}$ of a unit

Transformation   the movement of a shape by translation, reflection or rotation

Value   the value of a digit is given by its position

Vertex   a corner of a shape

Volume   of a solid or shape is the amount of space it fills or occupies.